Chanel
key collections

hamlyn

Chanel
key collections

Melissa Richards

Publishing Director:
Alison Goff

Executive Editor:
Mike Evans

Editor:
Humaira Husain

Art Director:
Keith Martin

Executive Art Editor:
Mark Winwood

Picture Research:
Wendy Gay

Production:
Louise Hall

With thanks to William Polk Carey, without whom much of this research would not have been possible, Stephane Houy-Towner at the Irene Lewisohn Library, Metropolitan Museum, NYC and to Marika Genty at Chanel, Paris.

The publishers wish to thank Chanel for their help and cooperation in the research and production of this book.

First published in 2000 by Hamlyn an imprint of Octopus Publishing Group Limited, 2–4 Heron Quays, London E14 4JP

ISBN 0 600 59726 1

A CIP catalogue record for this book is available upon request.

Produced by Toppan Printing Co Ltd
Printed in China

Christian BERARD

Biography

The best known and most often quoted story about Gabrielle Chanel is the one in which the Duke of Westminster asks her to marry him and she turns him down, saying: 'There have been many Duchesses of Westminster, but there is only one "Coco" Chanel.' It is funny, it is true and it says so much about the icons of our age – their cultural potency is that they are unique and we will never see their like again.

Chanel was an extraordinary character. Her contribution to 20th-century fashion is immense, and her life and the lives of those around her have helped to shape the way we feel about our times. She helped to change the way women felt about their bodies, their new-found freedom and sexuality, and was a living example to those who aspired to wear her fashions, which came to represent the truly independent, modern woman.

She was the quintessential example of her own look, right up to her death and she continues to influence the House of Chanel today. As even now, Karl Lagerfeld uses elements and aspects of her life in his contemporary creations, so that her spirit lives on.

She was a woman whose life was shaped in many ways by men: her feckless father, who abandoned her to a convent after the death of her mother; the officers who called her 'Coco' because of the only songs she knew, 'Qui qu'a vu Coco' and 'Ko Ko Ri Ko'; her lover Etienne Balsan, whose demi-mondaine lifestyle at Royallieu educated her in the ways of the world, though he did not include her in it; Boy Capel, whose money provided her with the means to prove herself as a businesswoman; Bend'Or, the Duke of Westminster; Iribe, the great artist and political nationalist; and countless other icons of the 20th century, whom she treated as equals.

Much is made of Chanel's attitude to her poor origins and of her liaisons, but these were the factors that shaped her taste and style. Her abhorrence of the trappings of middle-class pretensions and her appreciation for simplicity combined with grandeur can be traced back to her convent days.

Always the poor relation in her youth, Gabrielle transcended the cultural ideas of society by befriending artists, clients and other powerful men. At the time, dressmakers and tradespeople were generally kept at arm's length but, due to her association with the avant-garde and the calibre of her lovers, She created a unique position for herself. Few have known the type of luxury and wealth that Chanel did; fewer still have made such a stellar journey in social terms. No one could behave with such nonchalance or resourcefulness in the face of it but her. After all, who else would refuse to join the Chambre Syndicale? Or turn down the Legion d'Honneur? Or throw a large emerald into the sea in defiance?

There has rarely been a time when the Chanel look has not been appropriate or fashionable. How many other designers could boast the same? During her lifetime, she achieved a wider and longer lasting international fame than any other fashion figure in history. Although she consorted with some of the best-known figures in art, fashion and politics, she was always true to herself and held her own in the most extraordinary way for a woman in a male-dominated century. Her achievements were outstanding, even for today; freedom and daring were innate to her character and most of her maxims are clever statements of her desire to turn tradition on its head. She was helped by changing attitudes, when Syrie Maugham told Lord Berners that she could not entertain her seamstress, referring to Chanel, it was Maugham who appeared old-fashioned and prissy.

At her atelier, Chanel presided over both male and female staff, collaborating with men of ideas such as Iribe and aristocratic jewellery designers of her choice, ordering and shouting at her premières, admonishing models for not being able to match her stamina and criticising workmanship endlessly. Although Chanel may have indulged her favourites and taken her role as personal advisor to her clients extremely seriously, she was not really interested in other women. 'Women cannot be friends, you can love them or hate them, but you can never like them,' she stated. Nor were her classless attitudes quite compatible with her treatment of her staff. She never paid them very well and, during the general strike in France of 1936, organised by the Popular Front and led by friend Jean Renoir and others, Chanel simply did not understand the grievances of her workers and only capitulated to their demands for the good of the collection. Tales about her generosity to artists and friends are legion, but her kindness often amounted to the concept known today as 'tough love'. She usually interested herself in the talented and artistic. Loyalty too, was of great importance.

At the end of her life, journalists loved to describe Gabrielle Chanel as an outrageous old lady, wearing her boater and boots, theatrically cantankerous, cutting away with her famous scissors that were always suspended around her neck among the ropes of pearls, while she made mischief with her armoury of aphorisms about life, couture and those she had known. Her incisive wit and realism made her supremely quoteworthy. She also spoke in a long monotone with flat intonation, which many people found both distinctive and enthralling.

What a journey from the dreamy looking young woman whose column-long neck and austere clothes made a serene and striking picture of beauty, while she devoured cheap novels about girls who married into the aristocracy from humble origins. She always retained her slender, supple body and she maintained that the body was more important to her than the face: 'An ugly woman with a bright mind can turn herself with make-up into a "jolie-laide" ... clothes will do the rest.' True to these maxims, she always wore perfect make-up every day; lipstick, powder and a little subtle eyeshadow. However, for true beauty she maintained that 'a woman needed the look of love in her lover's eyes'.

Chanel delighted in pithy aphorisms for the press but, in hindsight, her style became synonymous with an intellectual outlook, for she was an extremely well-read autodidact and was associated with intellectuals and artists. It shows in the uncompromising nature of her style. It is hard to overstate the impact that Chanel had on modern clothing and, in particular, on jewellery. Many of the ideas she produced have become the very lynch-pin 20th-century aesthetics. She had the genius and unique talent to create and devise her own vocabulary of accessories, the inspiration to transform the lives of women through their clothing and the audacity to put very rich women in clothes inspired by the habits and simple vestments of nuns. The Chanel legacy is testimony to her strength of character, which has guaranteed that the ciphers and symbols so beloved by her continue to have such potent currency in the fickle world of fashion today.

Most of Chanel's signature elements were the culmination of her own experience: the braid is the result of living in a garrison town; the hard-edged red lips is the hallmark of a particular style of French *vendeuse*; the almost pathological neatness is one of the virtues learned at the convent. Her chic and much admired living style at La Pausa, her villa in the South of France, took its spareness from the simplicity of the convent, where light and shade accentuated the grandeur of architectural proportions. The paring down of, and emancipation from, the trappings of wealth and age are hallmarks of the 20th century but were taken into the world of fashion by Chanel. She hated the bourgeois lifestyle with all its trappings and in particular the way that the status of kept women was emphasised through their clothing.

Despite several monumental love affairs, Chanel did not find a lasting attachment. It must have been painful to take stock of the fact that she had no one to whom to leave her estate but her servants and business associates, having gradually distanced herself from her remaining family.

Gabrielle was such a perfectionist and yet such a realist that she earned huge respect from other talented people. 'She has more sense than any other woman in Europe,' Picasso said of her. Chanel wanted women to feel that her clothes were worth the price paid, even if the women were paying handsomely for them. Although most geniuses do not receive their due in monetary terms, she always insisted on full payment for a job done. She was reluctant to dress royalty: 'Those princesses and duchesses ... they never pay their bills. Why should I give them something for nothing? No one ever gave me anything.' Later, she declared: 'Fashion is not an art, it is a business.' Her relationship with her clothes was also curiously impersonal; once an article of clothing was finally finished, she never looked at it again.

The House of Chanel is now owned by the Wertheimer brothers, who had originally taken over the distribution of Parfums Chanel back in 1924, when the Chanel shops could no longer cope with the fast growing demand for scent. Their family company, Bourjois, took over the manufacture of Chanel No 5 and made it into a legend. Today, the House of Chanel is a world famous and institution.

The other beneficiaries of Chanel are those with a love of fashion, who interpret the significance of the changes in shape and attitude as well as how clothes are fashioned from the events of this extraordinary era, and who value the strength of an independent, strong spirit in a world of followers.

Many women, even today, are inspired by Gabrielle's astonishing sense of self. There are also those who daily buy into the heritage with every handbag, lipstick or nail polish. Indeed, everyone who wears modern western clothing is influenced by Chanel, whether it be a raincoat, a sweater or a pair of trousers.

The events of Chanel's life were hard and sad in many ways. Perhaps influenced by her stagy self-awareness, Chanel was a 'naughty child' who told people off, playing to the gallery of press. She often refused important guests admission to her shows, and took others in confidence, when they had clearly been warned off personal conversation by her staff. One gets the impression that, for Chanel, feeling loved was, in the end, being admired from afar, whether by the wearers of her couture or those who bought the cheap imitations – 'Let them copy my ideas, they belong to everybody. I refuse no one inspiration from them,' she declared with confidence.

There is a conflict in Gabrielle in that, while she claimed she always dressed women for seduction, she gave the impression that she did not feel loved herself. 'I never looked so much for someone to love, as for someone to love me,' she once said. However, her hard exterior, her wariness, her high expectations and the emptiness surrounding her in later life all suggest that few would have dared to try to get close to her.

Chanel's belief in romance was so strong that she constantly encouraged her models and protégés to find it wherever they could, and her belief in the strength of both love and sex gave her an insight into the factors of attraction and how women could look. That she successfully achieved independence of spirit and means, with charm and beauty, clearly shows that she wanted others to do so, too.

Gabrielle Chanel alone was addressed as Mademoiselle until she died – and even after her death – unlike most other women of a certain age in France. She remained eternally youthful and conspiratorial on the subject of life, despite the fact that she was well into her 30s when she made a name for herself and almost 90 when she died in 1971. Chanel remained indeed as ageless as the clothes she produced, and as girlish underneath it all as her protégés themselves.

Mademoiselle Chanel's apartment in the rue Cambon remains as she left it. A public place (she always slept at the Ritz), it contains many symbols of the extraordinary life of this larger than life character. Each of her belongings holds a significance in the marvellous story of her life. The large mirror hanging in the entrance hall with the two eagle heads has a central glass panel that is the same shape as the face of Chanel watches; it is also the same shape as the Place Vendôme.

Her chair and sofa are there, waiting as if, for one last time, Chanel might return to pose for a photograph. The Coromandel screens show her love of the orient and for Eastern philosophy, which she learned through Boy Capel and his business dealings in the East. The camellias resonate with associations with Chanel. The apartment is resplendent with antiques from the 16th, 17th and 18th centuries, many of them being keepsakes from admirers such as Giacometti, who made a hand sculpture for Chanel, and Stravinsky, who gave her a painting in gratitude for help with *Rites of Spring*.

The sheer number of leather-bound books shows that she was a formidably intelligent and self-educated woman. The sign of Leo, the crystal ball and her tarot cards, all left casually on her desk alongside her sunglasses, indicate her superstitious nature, as do the wheat, symbolising fertility and plenty after an early life full of privations and poverty, the frogs to attract well-being and joy, and the glittering chandelier perhaps made by her own hand with the metal G, interlocking Cs and No 5, possibly assembled after a trip to Venice with Misia and José Maria Sert.

In the grandly-furnished dining room, a 12-panel screen, unusual in its magnitude, sets off a heavy table and the pair of tables adapted by Chanel, with stands depicting food and wine personified. Over them hang mirrors with glass flowers refracting the light and creating more light and shadow in a way that puts one in mind of Chanel clothes: heavy, simple lines with light relief in the form of embellishment, jewellery and braid.

The animals in the apartment are usually in pairs, emphasising her solitude; the Madonna and child, and the Abbé and cross reflect her upbringing in the convent. The Madonna is a copy of one at Aubazine, which is identical but for one small detail – Chanel's Madonna has a rope belt, just like the chain belt she designed. The three boxes given to Chanel by the Duke of Westminster – silver on the outside, gold vermeil within – represent the central ethos of this remarkable style originator: *luxe caché*. For Chanel, whatever was on the outside, the real luxury was always hidden within.

The one addition to the apartment is Chanel's work chair, which was exceptionally low so she could check hems. This plain chair, its leather seat almost worn through, is the sole reminder of the fact that the ruler of this empire worked hard for a living. Then, just outside the door is the step on that famous mirrored staircase where she sat to gauge the reaction to her shows, surveying the scene as it unfolded to the press. She used to watch like a lone star, unseen. Perhaps she still does.

La pauvreté de luxe

...1916

In 1916, Gabrielle Chanel presented her first real collection – *La pauvreté de luxe* – she was 33 years old and knew how to attract attention. Originality was a shrewd and unexpected weapon in the world of fashion at this time, and the straightforward directness and practicality of what Mademoiselle Chanel had to offer proved deeply desirable.

Chanel had already received enviable press coverage for her millinery and fashion activities: Cecile Sorel and Gabrielle Dorziat were both endorsing her clothes; Sem had identified her with *le vrai chic* in his famous picture; and *Femina* magazine had featured the interior of her shop in Deauville in 1913. In July 1915, *Harper's Bazaar* showed a 'charming chemise' by Chanel; the fluidity of its design and narrow sash around the hips were signs of things to come. She took the emphasis away from the waist, where it had been for centuries, and made padding, frippery and folly redundant. This, and her knowledge of the possibilities of fabric, were the secrets of her success.

The basic shape of the chemise was to stay with Chanel throughout her career. Even when many other designers used the diagonal line over the body, she always kept to the ruthless dynamic between vertical and horizontal and a perfect fit.

The hallmarks of Chanel's style and ideals are evident in her first collection. Her clothes were made to make women look young. Her evening dresses were supremely feminine, in accord with the times and came with matching scarves of gossamer lightness. The timeless uniform of skirt and jacket in jersey and, later, colourful tweed is still worn the world over.

The fashion designer Poiret dubbed Chanel's clothes '*la pauvreté de luxe*' – a backhanded if apt compliment, as the luxurious details of her clothing, such as sable lining or a silken bodice, were hidden under an unassuming guise of rebellious spontaneity.

From this moment on, Chanel's reputation was guaranteed in the United States and Europe. Her great strength was that she was both a perfectionist and a realist; she had style but she also knew what was possible and what was not. In taking women out of stays and uncomfortable accessories, and encouraging them to feel in control of their own bodies, Chanel enabled women to move freely, day or night.

Chanel engendered the idea that clothes should be like a second skin, always comfortable whatever the wearer was doing. She encouraged women to choose what suited them, rather than slavishly follow unflattering trends. Ignoring the outré clothes chosen by sportswomen at the time, which she felt put women into the realm of the ridiculous, Chanel took ideas from both male garments and children's wardrobes to achieve the new prized possession: youth.

By the time of her first full collection, Chanel had achieved something no other designer had before: a total look. She borrowed elements of male dress and added girlish details to create a subtle but daring allure. Chanel style was a balance between clarity and whimsy, modesty and freedom.

The first collection designed by Chanel was unveiled in the resort town of Biarritz on the Atlantic coast of south-west France. Biarritz was a playground for the wealthy, where the English community had always enjoyed parading their finery, and many wealthy women had gone there to escape the privations of war. The collection was an immediate and astonishing success. Chanel's timing was perfect, for although the women residing in the town were not actually seeing any war action like their city counterparts, they wanted to buy into the style of their sister warworker, which represented a new vision of necessity and freedom of movement.

The brisk climate in this dramatic part of the Atlantic coastline encouraged this new look of English-inspired golf ensembles, stableboys' sweaters and practical knitted jersey skirts, whose brevity suited the social climate, too. The tradition has endured; even today, Biarritz is full of smart sailorwear and shops selling the big name luxury *marques*.

In various reminiscences, Gabrielle Chanel exclaimed that she could have sold a particular jersey over and over again. It was a customised version of a working man's sweater; she cut the neckline low and slashed down towards the chest, with a ribbon threaded through impromptu buttonholes. By borrowing from a man's wardrobe with a 'needs must' attitude, she succeeded in encapsulating a spirit of daring. Her adaptation of workclothes to suit the wealthier clientele of couture was another theme that stayed with Chanel throughout her career, always serving her well. Later, she would adapt the ideas of street gangs like the 'Apaches' in Paris and put society matrons in replicas of their unofficial uniforms and colours.

Any form of ostentation was ill-matched with the wartime spirit of denial, so Chanel's ethos was quickly identified with the feeling of the age. It is said frequently of Chanel that she alone was ready for the changing world during and after the war.

Chanel 'invented' the pleated skirt for women. 'Pleat by pleat ... persists in taking matter that is too beautiful only the very little that is suitable for elegance. She knows better than anyone elegance means sacrifice,' said an American essayist 40 years later.

For the 1916 collection, Chanel ordered the jersey from Rodier, a local clothmaker whose fabric had more usually been used for men's hosiery and underwear. The fabric was of no use to him because it could not be used as war issue, but Chanel saw that it had the correct weight to make a body-hugging suit with exactly the right movement. She used it to make a wonderfully modern khaki suit that had pockets and revers like a man's army jacket and a shortened skirt. Chanel continued to make these suits during the war and, in 1917, they appeared in different muted colours, with embroidery or a little fur trim – very sparingly used in contrast to the overbearing display of furs that was a feature of Edwardian clothing.

In the Ready to Wear collection for 1998, a modern version of this khaki jersey jacket has appeared in many magazines. It is unusual for modern designers to revisit this metamorphic period in fashion history – it is more usual to focus on lush Edwardian

femininity or the faster pace of the 1920s. However, it serves as a milestone for the House of Chanel and invites a comparison with the uncertain period of the 1910s before the fashion revolution gained momentum, showing us how far we have come since then and indicating how much further the House of Chanel intends to take fashion in the new millennium.

Some of the dresses from 1916 also featured an embroidered cardigan-shaped overhang, another detail that made Chanel's clothing less formal and more jaunty. The cardigan is always of singular importance in the work of Chanel, since it was a device that could be used to make formal clothes more casual. The device of a large collar and belt was similar to the clothes Chanel wore herself, though she often dressed in a longer, slimmer, straighter skirt – similar to those that appeared in the 1998/99 Autumn collection – to emphasise her physique.

To many rich women, the charm of Chanel lay in the fact that they could dress themselves in her clothes without help from a maid. There were no minute buttons to create dependence on others and no need to spend all day getting ready. These women also enjoyed wearing simple dresses whose luxury lay in the small touches – a sable lining where no one could see it, for example, or a Chanel label. Chanel had succeeded in creating important clothing with no pretensions.

Chanel's independent spirit and her wish to confront hypocritical social values continued to steer her away from the 'kept woman' look that she so despised. When the flapper look caught on, she, inevitably became its natural leader. Early on, her designs were simple and chic, but no different to those of Callot, Vionnet, Patou and Lanvin. In fact, many of their clothes were more interesting in construction than hers. However, the aspects of her competitors' clothing that made them interesting in their era are also the features that keep them tidily in their time. In comparison, the influence of Chanel on 20th-century fashion is almost impossible to overstate. Her ideals underpin all modern clothing, which is why her themes continue to be reinvented in endless permutations.

Like Poiret, Chanel produced a 'total look', of which she herself was the perfect example. Her style was always consistent – the same signature elements are still used today by the House of Chanel – but it is also a living, changing language, though one that remains instantly recognisable.

Chanel had a strict philosophy on the use of colour; she only employed the colours found in nature. There was also an obligatory attitude to go with the clothes, based on the often quoted Beau Brummell theory that the clothes must seem to be of the least importance. This and the borrowing of workclothes, uniforms and gentleman's apparel are still a textbook formula for fashion editors today. Simplification and dressing down have become the basis for all modern clothing at every price level. That is why it is easy to underestimate the effect the very early clothes of Chanel now found in museum collections had in their time; They seem so uncomplicated, compared to clothes by other couturiers, because Chanel wanted the emphasis to be on the wearer. Their ordinariness is a testimony to their revolutionary design.

After many centuries of texture, embellishment, padding and detail in fashion, Chanel started a century's habit of paring down. She designed straight-cut clothes, woollen suits with cardigan jackets and pleated skirts that were comfortable and easy to move in. Deceptively simple, they were for rich women who wanted simplicity and perfection in every detail.

Fitting on the body was the way that Chanel worked. Each garment was a painful process of building up and unpinning, until it was ready to be given to a seamstress for the tiniest stitches and highest quality workmanship. Physical fitness was a necessity in order to wear the clothes, and Chanel herself was a perfect example of discipline and posture. She had jersey fabrics specially woven for suits, usually in grey and beige, that she lined with fine silks, edged with luxurious braiding and trimmed with gorgeous buttons. The modesty of the colours, the girlishness of the length and details such as flirtatious neck bows belied the superb craftsmanship and quality of these garments.

Not surprisingly, Chanel's clothes translated particularly well across the Atlantic, becoming the successor to the tailormade tradition for serious, practical women who wished to seem independent but wealthy, young but knowledgeable, and from a puritan tradition but with a sporty lifestyle and a healthy appetite for flirtation and fun. This success was to be further amplified in the years to come.

No other couturier has imposed her personality so indelibly on any epoch. Chanel's commonsense and vision have outlasted all the whims and caprices of the fashion world throughout the 20th century and continue to challenge the received ideas in fashion in the new millennium.

Chanel simplified the shape of formal day wear, using sports influences, which belie the fabrics and detail. Fur is used as lining and appears discreetly at the neck and hem, its earlier function, as status symbol is deliberately rejected.

LA PAUVRETÉ DE LUXE / 1916

THIS PAGE *The layered coat and fur-trimmed wrap coat, luxuriant fur neck wrap with exaggerated shape black hat. Less is more in hats, simple dress shape and slimmer, with pearls and a sporty tweed suit, all hallmarks of Chanel style from 1916 on.*

OPPOSITE *(l–r) Luxuriant evening fabric made up into an unusual bathing dress shape. Charmeuse dress has cardigan over-hang with fur trim. 'The American cowboy' black satin coat fringed with black silk and handkerchief tie.*

The Duke of Westminster collection

...1925/26

Gabrielle Chanel probably did more for fashion during the 1920s than any other clothes designer. The style of the 1920s was emblematic of an attitude of mind and indicative of social change – a woman could be defined quite simply by what she wore. Wearing Chanel's clothes definitely required a new attitude. Social changes were occurring daily, so it must have been particularly exciting to dress up and act differently from the way that women had in the past – whether assuming the role of artful dodger or girlish prankster – while secretly wondering where it all might end.

The body was always all-important to Chanel's clothes which were sensuous and bold with no excesses. However, the simple lines of the clothing completely belie the ingenious construction of each garment. Unlike other designers, Chanel was as true to flapper ideals for evening wear as for daywear. For Chanel, it was the total image from head to toe that was important – the garçonne haircut, and the co-respondent shoes as well as the splendidly modern, feminine clothing. Christian Dior said of Chanel: 'With a black pullover and 10 rows of pearls, she revolutionised fashion.'

Paris reigned supreme in the fashion world of the 1920s, and Mademoiselle Chanel's reputation was particularly resonant across the Atlantic, where the spirited mix of modernity and youth was popular in the go-ahead ethos of the United States.

American *Vogue* pictured the collections for 1925/26 as a crowd of paper dolls on board an ocean liner with captions underneath, making much of the foreignness of these modish ideas. The captions feature all the designers of the day, with a higher proportion of Chanel models pictured than those of other designers. Although, the silhouette of the 1920s was simple, Chanel always contrived something extra, something subtle; in short, something characteristic of her *luxe* cachet.

The little black dress that she had invented became so ubiquitous in the 20s that *Vogue* christened it 'The Ford', after the latest standardised motor car that was being churned out on the American giant's production line. Chanel's production was prolific, too, but each creation was an agonising process. Although the shape of clothing at this time was straight and did not have to fit the contours of the body, it still had to accentuate the figure and move properly.

The 'Ford' dress, featured in 1926, was allocated a full-page spread in *Vogue*. The model wore a startling 'shingle' hairstyle that resembled the 'coconut cut' worn by Josephine Baker, which was incredibly daring at the time. With long sleeves, a slash neck and short skirt, the dress had very little decoration except for an integral diagonal cross of pintucks across the whole body, starting at the bodice and going across the skirt to accentuate the sinuous, slim shape.

Georges Lepape declared the future of fashion to be in sportswear; Patou and Lanvin both had sports lines in the 20s but relaxed into tea gowns and picture dresses for evening wear. Chanel designed evening pyjamas and trousers, and her evening dresses were made in deep, intense, plain fabrics that had sumptuous textures and gave an emphasis on movement.

The introduction of English tweeds for women was a new idea. Chanel made a feature of the lines and patterns of traditional fairisles as well as other knitting devices such as zigzags, which she also employed in sequinned evening wear. These patterns became more outré through the 20s, as Chanel became more involved in patronage of the arts and influenced by Cubism and Fauve colours.

Her racy sports whites and shorter pleated skirts were ideal for those who exercised, but Chanel's clothes were always merciless to the fuller form and she despised corsets. Pictures of Chanel and her friends wearing these tweeds and whites in natural settings or leaning on the deck of a yacht are so modern and unpretentious in pose and setting that they could be from fashion shoots now. Chanel herself, pictured sitting on a beach or a hill, looks tall, slim and radiant, but also clean and crisp, the lines of her outfits long and lean. They have the dimensions and physical attitude of modern clothes. Many other women's clothes of the 1920s are small and wide, but exhibits of Chanel in museums were originally made for tall, thin women.

Despite the popularity of the tan, upper class women still wore gloves, to distinguish them from those who laboured with their hands. Chanel's gloves were always interesting, as were her handkerchiefs and triangular scarves (worn by war workers for practical reasons and hijacked by Chanel). She also 'invented' slingback shoes and charm bracelets.

The most audacious invention and biggest signature statement for her clothes was the costume jewellery with which she accessorised it. During this period, achieving the total look meant wearing masses of 'junk' jewellery as well as real pieces. Chanel designed stupendous creations in *pâte de verre* that were then made up by Suzanne Gripoix to imitate pearls.

Since Chanel actually did own some highly important pieces of jewellery of her own, she loved to keep people guessing. However, for most women it was a big step to wear fake jewels, particularly such opulent-looking creations. Studied nonchalance was the key; if women were to break the hitherto unspoken rule that wearing jewels by day was vulgar, those jewels had to be huge and teamed with clothes that made the wearer look sweet and innocent. Typically, Chanel wore hers not only with suits and dresses, but she would also provocatively flaunt the grandest and most Baroque designs with baggy cotton trousers and beach suits.

Black and white became another Chanel trademark. She later described this complete absence of colour as 'perfect harmony'. It was also an easy way to teach women the principles of her disciplined approach to dressing and, of course, it was impossible to go wrong in monochrome.

The clothes that survive from this collection are varied but consistent in certain elements. Two day dresses in the Metropolitan Museum in New York look very simple; *faux* suits in

palest peach and beige, they have false 'jacket' pieces edged with tiny but deep pleats, and the details follow around to the seams and edges. On each dress, the hem appears to continue along the vertical seam, which has a minutely pleated border for emphasis, echoing the clever 'jacket front'. One of them has a climbing spiral effect, with the emphasis placed on the hips and legs, a device she later used for evening wear. Both dresses are made of the finest skin-coloured silk and, on examination of the inside, there is hardly a tell-tale sign that this spiral detail exists – one cannot see a stitch, nor any sign of the added weight of the tucks. In her 1960s clothes, Chanel quite often made a suit ensemble as a 'one-piece' and jacket, for brevity and to make the clothes fit the body and hang in a superior manner.

Coat dresses became the answer to the lean silhouette. For evening wear, though, black satin and dull gold quilting was a sophisticated idea, with a border of broadtail cloth. Chanel had recently designed a sofa in beige quilted suede, which is still in her apartment, and this design was also the basis for her bags and the whole matelassé idea, now found on everything from shoes to precious metal watchbands. Feathers and fur were other devices she used for borders on coats and evening clothes to create luxury without heaviness.

The midnight blue georgette crepe day dress – which featured gold embroidery, seed pearls and coloured jewelled stones in a motif designed for Chanel by the Grand Duchess Marie of Russia from a beautiful necklace belonging to the Romanov family – shows how the fusion of dark and light and the crossover of couture and jewellery was at work in her designs.

Wings and scarf-like attachments were always integral to the garments, and gossamer layers and flat bows were common decorative elements, again integral to a seam or construction element, then finally allowed to hang or float free. One exquisite evening dress in primrose silk at the Metropolitan has shoestring straps and a simple bodice and is narrow around the hips. Under the derrière, however, the seams become knots of the same fabric and streamers hang down the skirt. This has the effect of making the bottom seem tiny and taut, and the floating ends accentuate the vertical length of the leg with unparalleled elegance.

The top and bottom of a pair of pink pyjamas are each like the calyx of a flower, with petals of magenta,

OPPOSITE *Women were enjoying dressing up in mannish tweedy tailoring to go to winter racing and spectator sports.*

ABOVE LEFT *The relaxed effect of this sporty outfit belies the sheer intricacies of its construction and detail.*

LEFT *The more dressy evening version of the little black dress.*

RIGHT *With the shortest shingle, the lowest-cut back – this* Vogue *illustration caused a huge stir in its day.*

OPPOSITE BELOW *Scarves and flounces were used to create a feeling of constant movement and made a 'shimmy' inevitable, even at walking pace.*

OPPOSITE ABOVE *The famous 'Ford' dress, so-called because it was seen everywhere.*

RIGHT *The midnight blue and gold trompe-l'oeil dress, based on a design by Grand Duchess Marie of Russia, inspired by a real Romanov family necklace.*

OPPOSITE *Chanel's intricate construction of streamers and folds changed the way women moved at night, in contrast with big, easy styling by day.*

34 **THE DUKE OF WESTMINSTER COLLECTION / 1925/26**

Arthur O'NEILL

OPPOSITE *The geometric panels and side buttons illustrate the detail underlying the immediate uncomplicated impression given by Chanel's clothes.*

LEFT *Close to nakedness – shimmering spangles on a sinuous flesh-coloured background, gives a feeling of movement and grace.*

STEICHEN

OPPOSITE *Lady Diana Cooper, in a checked day-suit contemplates her tableau-image as the Madonna in thoroughly modern get-up.*

LEFT *Dressing down became imperative for appearances on the smartest yachts. The cardigan jackets and pleated skirts became ubiquitous.*

Shooting stars

...1932/33

At this stage in her life, Chanel was a woman of substance – she could go anywhere, entertaining royalty as well as statesmen while retaining her links with the '*beau monde*', and she had just been wooed by Hollywood. There was a hard-edged, professional glamour to her style; it was the perfect clothing for those women who possessed an independent spirit.

For economic reasons, classicism was entering the vocabulary of fashion swiftly and suddenly during this period. The constant hemline changes of the 1920s had meant that clothes dated quickly but, after the devastation of the Wall Street Crash, money now had to go further and quick changes in style could no longer be tolerated. Styles of dress immediately became more conservative and, for once, the effect was filtered up rather than down.

The rich, however, could still afford to travel to Paris for fittings. Nan Kempner, one of the few serious buyers of couture today, remembers going to fittings at Chanel with her mother during this period. Diana Vreeland, Mrs McCormick of the Chicago *Sun*, Laura Corrigan and Barbara Hutton were also insatiable buyers of clothes made by Chanel, and Violet Westminster was selling Chanel to London socialites.

Chanel's clothes were ideal for the department stores in America, who made them up from the 'line-to-line' dresses she sold them. Luckily for Chanel, she was relatively immune to the effects of the very high taxes on imports that were in place during the 1930s. For this reason, Chanel never advertised, so creating an even more exclusive image. Her clothes were of premium value to American women, and she greatly influenced many American designers, including Claire McCardell, Norman Norell and the French-born Pauline Trigere.

It goes without saying, of course, that Mademoiselle Chanel was also to influence all her main competitors at home in Paris, particularly at this time. In fact, so much so that the infernal problem of plagiarism that has dogged the house ever since started its serious effects at this time.

Delineator magazine ran this quite revealing copy: 'One can be jailed in France for copying a dress ... imagine the condition of our coat and suit industry if this principle were applied in America ... But whereas the models of the grandes maisons are carefully guarded from French manufacturers, they are sold quite freely to American copyists with the result that unless a French woman is quite fabulously rich so that she can buy grand couturier models, she can't ... keep up with fashion; but the American woman can, according to her purse, buy the French model, or a copy at any price from $300 to $30 and the excellence of the $30 model is amazing ... Take the winter collections, for example. Chanel, one of the most difficult to bend to the buyer's wishes, shows on August 5th. By the 22nd, she delivers her orders. A week later the models are in America and two weeks thereafter ... copies are ... in the shops.'

The trend for resortwear continued to grow, particularly in the United States, where several generations of informal sportswear manufacturers have been influenced by Chanel's daring practice of borrowing from the masculine repertoire of sportsclothes. Women loved outfits that accentuated their movement. Chanel gave them the confidence to borrow from the shopgirl, teaming unlikely items such as espadrilles with an abundance of fake or real jewellery.

For fashion, particularly sportswear, things would never again seem so effortlessly innovative. Despite the economic pressures during this period, this is the time when the principles of 'classic' fashion were first invented. Chanel's style now comprised a dramatic palette of luxuriant fabrics for evening wear; for daytime, tweeds in exotic colour combinations were modelled into lean and fluid lines, the rigorous tailoring a perfect showcase for her flawless workmanship.

The easy lines and the dramatic effect of monochrome palette is the key to the look, with the play on dark and light coming from the design. Simplicity, not austerity, was the foundation of Chanel's design values. As she soared socially, the less complicated everything seemed to become. The items of clothing she introduced include the peacoat, trench pants for getting in and out of Venetian gondolas and espadrilles for seaside donkey rides. Having worked with dancers and knitted clothes for *Le Train Bleu* in 1924, Chanel now had a better idea of how the female body moved than almost any other couturier. Her easy lifestyle at La Pausa, in the South of France was also noted; freedom was the luxury that everybody wanted.

Following the introduction of Mademoiselle Chanel in England, the Duke of Westminster allowed Chanel to use his house in Grosvenor Square to stage a fashion show in aid of charity. Chanel created 130 outfits made from British materials and, since these models were not for sale, she authorised her designs to be copied. This was a wise, headline-catching endeavour and was one of the factors that has made her ever-influential, since she never minded being imitated.

If her creations tended to be sporty or neutral for the daytime during this period, the story changed completely at night. She believed that women could be 'caterpillars by day and butterflies at night'. The collection's feather dress is almost organic in colour. Starkly simple at the top, it has a slash neck and long, slim outline down to the deep feather hem, made of whole, vertically hanging feathers, with plumes the same length. The unexpected thrill lies in the ingenious three-quarter length open 'plaited' sleeves, knotted at the bottom and with the ends hanging free.

Less obvious but no less intense is the sequinned dress designed for Loelia Ponsonby, who married the Duke of Westminster. With midnight blue sequins all over, it is gently bias cut with a low, V-necked tank top. There are no superfluous details. The seams once again form the decoration on the dress, as they cleverly entwine to form a bow at the low-cut neckline. The stitching serves to emphasise the form of the dress as it skims the body. The sequins are almost integral to the fabric and this effect was achieved on several dresses in this collection.

de Meyer

The Bendels dress and hat are more romantic, thanks to the restrained print and the length and generosity of the skirt. The hat and the dimensions of the dress are in perfect harmony, making it a timeless classic.

The Hoyningen-Huené wedding dress is a variation on the basic style of dress that she made for debutantes and society women at court. The skirt is perfectly straight and long, with no train and tiny buttons up the front. The perfection of the Chanel sleeve this time manifests itself in an elongated cuff, tightly buttoned until it flares out over the hand, stopping short of the fingers. The drama of this dress lies in the heavy richness of the duchesse satin, enhanced by the unusual arrangement of the delicate veil and the freshness of the circlet of orange blossom at the neck. The dress is the epitome of 1930s classicism.

Lots of tiny buttons up the front of the clothes is a strong feature of this collection. They appear in the lovely V-necked evening dress, advertised in both black and black-and-white chevrons, that has a 'waistcoat' effect over the torso. Two godets panels form the bottom of the waistcoat, which carries the buttons, and the skirt is gently folded into gathers over the stomach and draped into a sinuous form that flares out at the hem.

The flower dress that appeared in *Vogue* is unusual for Chanel, whose credo of elegance usually shied away from anything patterned that was not tweed or knitted. However, this ensemble shows her versatility. It is very feminine, subtle and it appeared in many different fabrics.

An article in the Chicago *Daily News* declared of her evening wear: 'Much silver in Mme Lanvin's fall creations; Chanel's favourite trim is gold. This year, Mademoiselle Chanel has become a formidable concurrente of the big material houses. Each manikin, whether in black, green, red, brown or blue, wore a card with the number of her model and the words *"tissus Chanel"*. Apparently her variety of fabrics was as numerous as Mme Lanvin's except that she added quantities of moiré and jerseys. The latter material she has been using for years. She uses them all so we can walk easily. The tendency was for the collared throat. For evening, the line was frequently off the shoulder and very becoming to youth. Her collection is the first ... that emphasised dresses becoming to the debutante ... True to the French financial policy, her favourite metal is gold.'

Chanel's fabric factory in Asniéres, opened in 1931, was the strength

HARLINGUE-VIOLLET

behind many of her collections. The tweeds and prints are outstanding in their innovative colour combinations and had the advantage of being made in relative secrecy. Her coat dress model was now imitated everywhere but, because Chanel owned a fabric factory, she could control the weights and colours of her creations precisely.

Unsurprisingly, the shape of suits in the collection veers towards longer, flared lines, to fit in with the concern for classicism. A beige jersey coat with a trim in brown astrakhan, a very important fur to Chanel, is a modest garment, contrasting sharply with the formal afternoon suit, which utilised the new heavy black blistered ciré satin for the blouse and teamed it with a 'nutshell' hat. The small waist makes a feature of the upper body, while the skirt and jacket mould the hips and follow into a long, lean line.

The Chanel suit during this period was the most formal item. Its short, fitted jacket with a military front and the slightly flared skirts lend a formal element not present in the evening clothes, which are deliberately casual and simple with the focus on the fabric and construction.

This collection's sportswear line was impressive, and the interface between sports and formal wear within it was to influence American designers strongly. For Chanel, an evening dress could be modelled on the same design as a beach dress, the different mood being conveyed entirely by the fabric. A famous Hoyningen-Huené picture shows the grandeur of a red-and-white beach dress with white organdie hat. The unique genius of the chevron arrangement and the cap sleeve that is created from the decoration on the bodice shows the inventiveness of its creator. Again, this dress could easily have been a dinner dress if it had been made in another fabric.

In changing the rules about when and where jewellery should be worn, and by making the wearing of fakes acceptable, Chanel had demonstrated the importance of artistry. She had daringly challenged the old notions of the importance of the actual jewels by placing a new emphasis on who designed them and who wore them.

Now Chanel set about applying her notions to more important stones. In 1932, she was asked by the Diamond Commission to create a collection of real jewellery.

These pieces were first seen on beautifully detailed mannequins rather than the usual blank velvet in a heavily guarded exhibition held in Paris in aid of charity. Iribe, already collaborating with Chanel and one of

Robert BRESSON

the great loves of her life, was the inspiration. She also wanted to portray the magic of jewels for women.

Chanel's connections with legendary artists and dreamers were evident in her designs for jewellery. These jewels were brilliantly conceived. As she said herself: 'My jewellery represents first and foremost an idea.' Each one was interchangeable, with discreet clasps or even none at all in the case of the comet necklace and diadem – with these pieces there was an infinite number of ways to display the dazzle of the diamonds, depending on the wearer's mood and ingenuity.

Each piece featured a large motif of stars, knots or feathers. They were modern in inspiration but also large, simple and graphic to ensure that they would suit all occasions. They were also easy to wear because they were able to move; they were designed to fit on the body and settle against the contours of the neck and head.

The graphic quality of these outsize creations, and the cut of the diamonds themselves, perfectly complemented the sculptural quality of 1930s coiffures and the simplicity of the clothes, which also relied on cut and quality for their effect. Some of the pieces were exhibited with furs.

Chanel's beautiful jewels were ideal for counteracting the gloomy effects of the Depression. Interestingly, when Gabrielle Chanel went to Hollywood, her costumes did not translate to the world of film because they were too low-key. However, if anyone had suggested taking these stunning gems to the silver screen, they were so grand that they would never have been believable. Sem said of them, with typical wit and incisiveness: 'At last we have the real imitating the artificial.'

For the few who could afford them, they were meant to constitute fantasy, larger than the humdrum escapism of Hollywood. The exhibition was in aid of a children's charity and it travelled abroad to raise funds, allowing people to see the jewellery.

Unlike the jewels 'of the rue de la Paix' despised by Chanel as the spoils of kept women, who wore their wealth on the outside with no sense of style, these jewels were flexible, adaptable and could be worn in many different ways, as Chanel herself liked to do. Chanel was constantly changing and adapting things – clothes, jewellery, fashions – but she always used the same principles to do so.

It was typical of Chanel to advocate less expensive fashion accessories that could be added freely to one's monthly account at the couturier's, and then to design such unearthly and startling creations that needed a monumental investment to acquire. Looking at Chanel in the 30s, one can see that she knew both sides of the market. She had become the embodiment of the modern and independent woman but she was generous to others. When she was a young woman, she had seen an older generation of courtesans, whose displays of trophies from admirers constituted their only provision for an uncertain old age.

Her costume jewels were easily the most controversial of her innovations, and she made a feature of them many times throughout her career. She created her owns designs in modelling clay and beads, and engaged Count Etienne de Beaumont to be in charge of her workrooms and designs. Called 'illusion jewellery', her creations were made of glass beads to resemble the real stones that Chanel possessed and adored. The beads were formed into large square-cut emeralds, pigeon-blood rubies and deep, dark sapphires. Fashioned into stupendous pendants and chains, these larger than life pieces were like a rare treasure trove. Of course, the more casual the clothing with which they were worn, the more breathtaking the effect.

Francois Hugo, great grandson of the poet and author, was engaged to design jewellery pieces for Chanel. Another very fruitful collaboration was with the Sicilian nobleman Count Fulco de Verdura. They created a collection of Baroque-inspired bracelets and other baubles, the best known of which were the bracelets bearing the Cross of Malta, which Chanel is seen wearing in some of her most famous photographs. Verdura left in 1934 to found the eponymous company, which is still in New York.

Mr Goossens and Madame Gripoix also worked with Chanel: both firms still supply the House of Chanel with fake jewellery pieces. The marriage of priceless and fake demonstrates her free spirit and ingenuity perfectly. Her own daring creativity inspired her customers to wear a look that has been current ever since its inception.

On taking stock of the magnificent gifts Chanel herself had received from Bend'or and her Romanov pearls, side by side with her fake jewellery designs, the only absolute rule that can possibly be divined is that there is no fake chic. Chanel wore her jewels for their aesthetic merit. She changed designs and reshaped the ideals of the modern woman in that she advocated wearing what brings out the best in the individual. The way she expressed it was: 'Luxury is not the opposite of poverty, it is the opposite of vulgarity.'

RIGHT *This tartan day dress has the formality of a suit, while its heavy studded belt gives it the androgymous resonance that fashion editors relish today.*

OPPOSITE *Demurely romantic, bare shoulders, high neck - this dress could have been worn for the next 70 years without being out of fashion.*

de Meyer

RIGHT *A schoolgirl tunic and tie and monochrome check lining become an elegant composition of dramatic contrasts.*

OPPOSITE *Princess Dimitri of Russia, photographed by Hoyningen-Huene in her heavy white satin wedding dress with a circlet of orange blossoms at the neck.*

de MEYER

HOYNINGEN-HUENE

RIGHT *'Butterflies at night' Very sculptural form to the capelet and hem insets, over the moulded sequin body of this evening dress.*

OPPOSITE *This striking black cire suit was made in several different versions. Strict, sharp tailoring is relieved and softened by the white hat.*

OVERLEAF, LEFT *Chanel's classic combination of white collar bow and cuffs on a nippy black suit with mannish hat.*

OVERLEAF, RIGHT *To achieve the perfect balance, it is essential to emphasise the female form with small shoulder and tight arms.*

Cecil BEATON

LUZA-MORAL

LUZA-MORAL

RIGHT *Gorgeous white lace with a nostalgic feel, hangs softly in layers and no padding ensures a willowy form.*

OPPOSITE *Riviera Chic – this bold chevron stripe dress features gossamer fine fabric and hat which could translate into evening wear.*

HOYNINGEN-HUENE

HOYNINGEN–HUENE

KERTESZ

LEFT *The jewellery exhibition raised considerable sums for children's charities and travelled to London and America. It was also reported to boost diamond sales in the US.*

RIGHT *The realistically detailed wax mannequins contrast with the huge fantasy-scale diamond creations.*

HARLINGUE–VIOLLET

RIGHT *'Some of my necklaces, following the shape of the neck, do not close; some of my rings coil up. 'My jewellery never stands in isolation from the idea of women and their dress'.*

OPPOSITE *A clever play on the function of the tiara and the fashion for the fringe. 'My jewellery represents first and foremost an idea.' Chanel.*

Robert BRESSON

Robert BRESSON

Frivolity – a serious business

...1937/38

Cecil BEATON

The 1937/38 fashion season witnessed the most lyrical and romantic period of Chanel's work. Women were beginning to tire of the disciplined, pared down looks of the early 1930s and were just beginning to enjoy a period of long-awaited economic revival, though it soon collapsed.

Images from the Regency period and the 19th century as a whole had a strong impact on the shapes of the clothes and furniture of the 1930s. For many people, this collection from Chanel seemed quite atypical. She was considered the least romantic of designers, but in this collection there is a great deal of 'frou frou' as well as influences from French traditional folk clothing, (white cotton and muslin dresses with colourful striped grosgrain sashes and black ribbons), such as she might have seen in her childhood, peasant clothes from all over the world, oriental jewellery and 'frou-frou' styles from another of her formative influences, the music hall.

While the collection may superficially seem to be a departure from Chanel's normal styles and designs, on close examination the clothes have all the familiar features: darkness relieved by light in all the usual combinations; simplicity and neatness for daywear; a unique brand of dressed-up informality for evening wear. Rather than traditional evening gowns, the evening look was defined by the shin-length skirts that were worn with blouses, which accentuated the witty shoe designs of the period.

Chanel's most brilliant stroke was the introduction of evening trousers in the guise of extravagant gypsy outfits. These allowed lovely, vibrant prints to be used together with huge sleeves, sashes and jewellery. When tempered by wide trousers and colourful headscarves, the overall mood was one of relaxed sophistication.

Despite a continuing trend towards the use of corsets by other designers, Chanel stuck fast to her principles and made the bodices of her strapless gowns with finer bones and weights. In the 1937 collection, the necklines become lacy and feature drawstrings. Colours are bright and patterns take hold, more often than not happily mismatched and bursting with a feeling of spontaneity.

The workmanship of these pre-war dresses is amazing; the tiny stitches, the silken pockets for weights, sawcut edges on chiffon, and hook-and-eye fastenings inside outer dresses are all superb. Many of these clothes, particularly the suits that worn by Diana Vreeland, look almost 1970s in style.

The suits' plainness is freshened with astrakhan trims, flowers and gloves for evening wear, or a simple dress. There are also more decorative garlands to relieve the heaviness, and classicism and sportiness can be seen creeping into the designs. Her lace dresses, with their youthful silhouette, show Edwardian influences.

Chanel's motivation for giving her clothes some touch of frivolity – apart from her instinctive and continuing feel for women's wishes – was that her nemesis, Elsa Schiaparelli, was now flaunting her own relationship with the artists of the day, serving up visual jokes and fantasy with a relentless inspiration. The press played on this rivalry and constantly invited comparisons between Chanel and Schiap.

At this time, Chanel's output was prolific and the wealth of accessories was vast. Women had evidently by now had enough of the cool glamour of the early and mid-30s and were demanding new fantasy elements in their fashion, with touches of whimsy and fun. Schiap was renowned for her surrealistic visual jokes and her cellophane jewellery; Chanel's approach remained different, as always. She had glamorised the links between art and fashion through her own example and through patronage of the arts, not through publicity. Since her earliest meeting with Misia Sert in 1917, Chanel had continuously financed numerous productions and events.

Chanel's suits had already featured surreal touches, such as fishscale sequins and a shell hat. Bénito, who loved to emphasise the colour and shape of his subjects, now produced a drawing of Chanel and Schiap dresses together that highlighted the surreal influences evident in both designers' work. The pictures of her designs by Christian Bérard show the clothes to their best advantage – elongated but curvaceous sylphs wearing outfits of complementary colours and patterns. Bérard had previously worked with Chanel's great friend Cocteau and, in March 1938, he put a Chanel dress in a Boucher context, adding considerably to the romantic overtones.

Brooches and jewels – delicately painted flowers and glass necklaces that 'you would think were globules of soap', wrote *Vogue* – were once again throwaway items. There was also a collection of jewellery photographed by Kollar in 1939, which clearly demonstrated the oriental influences in her jewellery at the time; it could easily be contemporary. Bérard also made some jewellery for Chanel.

Much of the 37/38 collection shows the influences that led Chanel to move towards the Winterhalter and Watteau feel that is said to anticipate the 'New Look', but without the Tricolore collection's intensely French nationalist feeling – that collection was more politically motivated, in a mood of defiance against the Germans. In a sense, therefore, the collection is purer in terms of Chanel style than the immediate pre-war models, which show a reaction against wearing the Tyrolean hats and suits that were fashionable elsewhere.

There was a lot of black and white in this collection. The famous 'Little Black Dress' assumes a white collar and cuffs during this period, a feature that was echoed in the 1978 shows.

For evening, the dominant shape was the hourglass, flaring out at the hem. This was achieved by wearing horsehair and stiffened petticoats. When Karl Lagerfeld chose this exact period as the inspiration for his first collection for the House of Chanel, he adapted this shape to create the 'windmill' skirt. On the surface it

François KOLLAR

seems an odd period to choose but, on reflection, it was a diplomatic way to take the fashions of the House of Chanel away from the influences of the old 70s shapes (often based on the 40s) and into his vision for the 80s. One can see through his work, as well as through the evidence from 1937, the truth of Chanel's comment that 'frivolity is a very serious business'.

The wealth of accessories to go with the clothes of the 1937/38 collection is prodigious. The tiny little hats – almost hairbands – feature excessive decoration, with huge black bows or piles of fresh white flowers to complement the froufrou evening dresses and suits. To increase the feeling of being dressed up, there are lots of beautiful gloves, all fabulous, all different. The gypsy clothes possess a distinctive impromptu mood, although the sashes and headbands are in reality carefully thought out pieces of whimsy that can simply be thrown on to produce a look of sophisticated glamour from head to toe with very little effort.

Chanel's own casual clothes seem to be more colourful at this time. They are meticulously reported in several *Vogue* articles about her long holidays in Capri, or at home at La Pausa in the South of France. Invariably she is shown wearing trousers, sometimes pink or white, teamed with striped tops, espadrilles and an alice band, which soon became almost obligatory after *Vogue* reported it.

The collection featured the black sequinned suit for Diana Vreeland, which is relieved by a red rose. There is also the deep red velvet suit created for Diana Vreeland, with its high Victorian collar and peplum contrasting with the suit's short length, and the navy linen suit with ribbing. These last two could easily have been designed in the 70s but are of 30s vintage. The suit of the Comeback collection in 1954 can be traced to this time and not the later, more dressy affairs that anticipate the New Look.

The trouser suit is the *pièce de résistance*, its triumph coming from the blending of dressed up and casual looks in Chanel's unique, revolutionary way. As with the evening clothes, it is the sequins and the necktie bows that transform the trouser suit into something all women could easily wear. The delineation of the body is made softer for evening and the stark white shirts against the face facilitate a feminine attitude. Diana Vreeland's sequinned suit is perhaps the best example of this pared down glamour; the cut and the fabric do all the work, without obscuring the presence of the wearer, who no doubt knew exactly how to carry it off to perfection. Its design was to be reincarnated several times by Chanel in the 1960s, when its appeal was universal and therefore copied indiscriminately by many.

The evening dresses shown in *Vogue* perfectly complemented the swept-up hairstyle that became the popular alternative to short hair during the war. Echoes of these dresses can be seen in the 1990s collections.

Chanel loved at this time to play with the pneumatic, womanly shape. She created exploding flounces at the hem; spiralled great white frills down the body; and highlighted the narrow curve of the hips and legs in much the same way as she had with her jacket dresses in the 1920s, but with infinitely more suggestive results. One evening dress for Diana Vreeland featured black sequins, red satin revers, a wide cummerbund and gathers.

There are also lace peasant dresses in the collection, with lots of white pintucks and traditional striped grosgrain belts. They feature a front neck panel, a rounded yoke, puffed sleeves, a small waist and a hem flounce.

These dresses are in the shape that is standard throughout the collection and it is reinterpreted constantly in black. It is also reminiscent of the style of dress that Chanel probably wore as a young *irregulière* in the music halls, where she sang and danced and earned her nickname 'Coco'. See-through sleeves and stoles complement these dresses.

Another feature of the collection is the fabulous star-spangled dark evening dress worn by Misia Sert in the famous photograph of her in 1937 by Francois Kollar. This lovely, long evening confection shows Chanel's genius to the full. The dress is elegant and lyrical with its large, bright stars, but also whimsical – never too much, but enough to be grand.

A marvellous series of designs from the time (said to have been drawn by her friend Christian Bérard)show all the famous signature elements of her individual style. In 1991, Lagerfeld reinterpreted these for inspiration. The drawings manifest so much from the 1930s period: the suits, the lucky numbers, the pearls, the jewellery and the bows, showing both whimsy and great discipline in equal parts.

After just one more collection, Chanel would shut up shop, leaving only her perfumes and accessories in Paris. Her Winterhalter suit was featured with a woman looking over a wall into a painted picture. It would be 17 years before Chanel showed her designs again – this time to a very different landscape indeed.

RIGHT *Shapely, suggestive and sparkling – women suddenly craved fantasy and fun. Pink and flesh tones were used often by Chanel to emphasise the new delicate glamour.*

OPPOSITE *Role play – this drapery has a strong Greco-Roman feel , worn with elaborate jewellery and hood, it could be a costume for a film.*

HORST

HORST

OPPOSITE *Music Hall influences are strongly stated in this backstage shot. The fitted bodice contrast at top with longest and tightest fingerless gloves and a slice of patterned net up the side.*

LEFT *Strong pattern and lightest, tightest tailoring contrast with chunky and dramatic costume jewellery and perky hat.*

NELSON

RIGHT *A fountain of miniscule width pleats in the same dress as formed bodice – a technical challenge perfectly executed.*

OPPOSITE *The emphasis on girlish nostalgic headwear and long, slim hourglass figure recall the naughty 90s.*

HORST

George PLATT-LYNES

RIGHT *After so much classic clothing, women suddenly yearned for fantasy and a spark of wit.*

OPPOSITE *Chanel's feeling for form was spot on when she mixed Cossack inspired furs with the exaggerated leanness of the pre-war suit.*

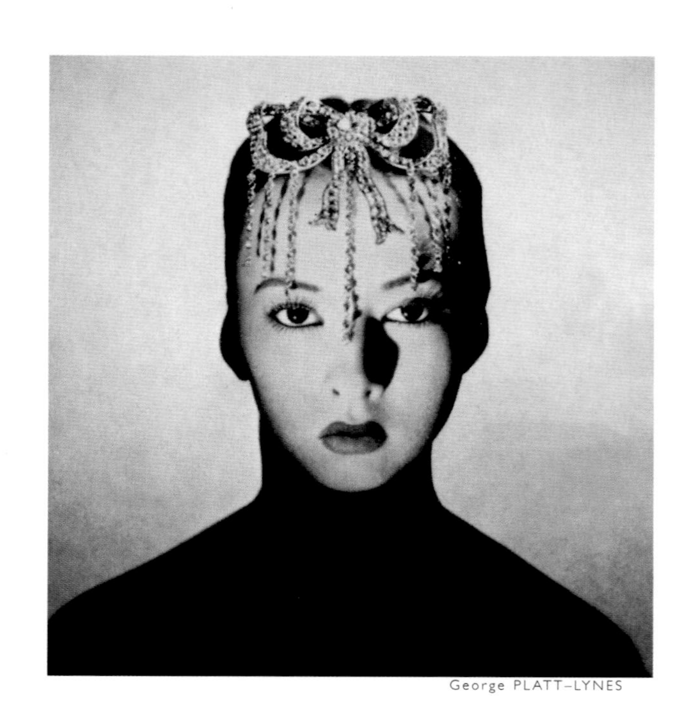

George PLATT-LYNES

HORST

HOYNINGEN–HUENÉ

RIGHT *Unlike other couturiers, Chanel did not use bodices for form, but relied on small weights, soft boning and posture.*

OPPOSITE *This famous photograph features the heavy green and red jewellery Chanel characterised and made into a signature element for her style.*

François KOLLAR

MAN RAY

LEFT *The peasant top and gathered skirt – made in similar, but different patterns to emphasise the informality of the two-piece evening outfits.*

RIGHT *Liquid gold – lamé evening suit with pleated skirt and jacket with fabulous hat and veil, intricate gold trellis belt and maltese cross bracelet.*

HORST

The Comeback collection

...1954

1954

E KAMMERMAN

'A long wait downstairs, and seating mix-ups when press and buyers were finally allowed up into the salon, gave the Chanel 1954 opening the air of the New York subway at rush hour ... Before the first model appeared everyone was irritated and the general attitude was: This had better be good – or else.'

Women's Wear Daily
February 8th, 1954

In typical Chanel fashion, the seats to the show were allocated to those she considered sympathetic and not in order of rank. At Chanel shows, it was long established that only those who were there on business ever sat down. Noses were put out of joint and egos were ruffled; because of some mishap, the *Times* correspondent was late and was refused admission. For a while it seemed foolhardy but Mademoiselle Chanel was to emerge triumphant.

It is well known that the reaction in many magazines to the Comeback collection was less than kind. Many fashion editors, like Carmel Snow of *Harper's Bazaar*, who was a complete devotee to Dior, did not even print pictures of the clothes. *Elle* and *LIFE* magazines, on the other hand, were given an 'exclusive interview' along with several other publications and were fairly complimentary. American retailers sensed that women might be ready for these easy clothes; buyers were eventually to prove them right and the harsher press coverage wrong.

The first model appeared wearing a cardigan suit in black jersey. Then came a series of suits with cardigan-style jackets and slender skirts of matching tweed or wool jersey, worn with the trademark shirts in white or prints to match the lining of the jacket. Some of the jackets had belts and many sleeves unbuttoned at the cuffs to show the lining. Coats showed the same lining as the dress print and one jacket had a curved seam under the bust, which had been a favourite Chanel feature before the war.

There were shirtwaisters with pleats and several dresses made in Bucol's new 'puckered' nylons; these dresses featured wide skirts, fitted bodices and open necklines. These revived Chanel's popular 1937 dinner length. There were, unsurprisingly at this time, no trousers in this collection.

Evening dresses were tight around the bust and hips and sprang out below; combinations of satin and tulle or sheer lace were common. They had no padding or stiffening and were flattering to women of any age. The embroidered, strapless evening dress, in a strong print and with a tulle skirt, was featured in *LIFE* magazine.

The most revolutionary shape lay in a tiered, full skirt coming out from a sheath dress, just like a drawing of a Christmas tree. It was black with roses poised on the outermost tip of each layer. This was intended for dinner or 'late afternoon'. It is an extraordinary concept, particularly coming from a couturier whose designs had hitherto been classical. There was little mention of this in the press, however.

The colours of the collection were mainly navy and black, enlivened by white for evening wear and pink and red for clothes in printed fabrics.

Chanel maintained that her reason for doing another collection at this time was boredom – 'Flee boredom, it's fattening' – and a wish to liberate women. *LIFE* magazine showed some clothes by her contemporaries, which, while exquisite, were impractical. This was the view of the retailers, whose experience told them that simplicity would be the way of the future. At this there was an explosion in number of 'young marrieds' and career girls, none of whom could probably sustain for long the corseted type of elegance required by the designs of some of Chanel's competitors. The thrill of dressing up in the New Look would soon pall and diverse images for women would take its place.

Chanel's jersey dresses were right for the moment, the crossover front making them less formal and plain. These clothes could stand alone like a piece of art that one could wear anywhere, just like the rediscovered jersey dresses of the 1998/99 collection. So many of Chanel's revolutionary garments have returned again and again over the years, from the pleated skirt and the trenchcoat to the charm bracelet. As she said: 'Fashion passes, style remains. *La mode* is made of a few amusing ideas, which are used in order to be used up and replaced by others in a new collection. A style should be preserved even as it is renewed and evolved.'

The shape of the suit, Chanel's most easily identifiable item, did just that. It continued to evolve and is still evolving today. Chanel understood then what women feel even more strongly now: they do not want a prescribed look; they want to feel comfortable and to wear clothes that are compatible with who they are.

The navy sailor suit, the most famous piece of this collection, looks for all the world like the Sunday best of a provincial schoolteacher. It cuts across the pretence and the artifice of the other Paris fashions, which put bones in tweed suits that were designed especially for cocktail parties. With its little straw boater and white muslin shirt, the sailor suit's modesty is quite incredible. It made an indelible impression at the time and one can imagine what a relief it was to cast off the New Look and to wear this easy garment in its place.

The suit's blouse has a pointed, turnover collar above a fly closing, which buttons under an applied band from the collar to the waistband. A

Paul HIMMEL

self-fabric band is set in at the shoulderline, ending in a pointed tab and buttoning at the top of each sleeve. These devices were employed by Karl Lagerfeld on the blouse for the sailor trouser suit in his 1983 collection. The blouse has set-in sleeves finished at the wrist with bias-cut turnback cuffs that fasten with metal links, plated in gold. They are a typical Chanel feature and, as usual, the links always work properly and are exquisitely turned. The cufflinks have flower-like shank buttons at the end of a metal loop and the flower shapes are decorated with four bands, thus dividing the flowers into quadrants.

Much of the feeling for what the suit represents is to be found in its shape. As Chanel used to tell journalists: 'A woman's shoulder is here [pointing at her own]. See how it comes forward slightly. That's why it is feminine and pretty. It is not like this [squaring her shoulders]. That's for a man. Look at the sleeve [dangling her own]. If it hangs well and the hands show well, all is well.'

The 'turtle suit' at the Metropolitan Museum in New York, also from 1954, is a more typical piece from the period. It makes certain concessions to the trends of the time but, ultimately, it is an eminently wearable ensemble that relies on the good figure of the wearer. It has little turtle-shaped buttons and crossover tabs on the jacket and shirt. This season's collection also featured a white wool suit in Chanel's classic style, with black and red trim.

As usual, Chanel was ready with some pithy quotes to go with the new direction in clothing. She made the point that there were 'too many men in couture now' and stated that it was 'the American penchant for comfort without *luxe*' that had spurred her on to create this collection.

Vogue ran a three-page article on February 15th, 1954, saying: 'Quite different from the Chanel in a jersey suit of red or beige, sparkling with jewels and chattering with her famous friends, is the Chanel at work. Then she wants to be alone. She is silent. She works with fabric on a live girl, moulding, pushing the model away, pulling her forward, slashing at the cut, changing the curve. On the day before the collection opening, a double ritual takes place. In the big salon, with the girls parading in front of her, Chanel lies flat on her stomach to see that the hems hang right. She orders boxes of flowers, ribbons, buttons brought in ready to be added if necessary. Instead of adding, she always takes way a detail already there. She unclutters the cluttered.'

Paul HIMMEL

Chanel expressed a strong desire to see women get back on track: 'I want women to look pretty and young. A dress should not be a disguise. If a fashion isn't taken up by everybody, then it is not a fashion but an eccentricity, a fancy dress. An eccentric dress does not make one an eccentric – a woman is dull in an eccentric dress if she is dull without it.' And again: 'Look for the woman in the dress. If there is no woman, there is no dress.'

Chanel's aversion to male couturiers was well known. While she believed in the ability of men to appreciate clothes, she felt that men were not able to design successfully for women. Before the war, the Parisian fashion world was dominated by women but now there were men, whose main aim was to get themselves noticed, rather than their clients. She knew what women wanted and how to give it to them: 'A dress must be made like a watch – if a tiny wheel does not work, make the dress or the watch over. A dress isn't right if it is uncomfortable.'

As well as dresses, Chanel offered women the quilted bag, as yet with no initials on it, and the two-tone shoes and hair bows that have become so much a part of Chanel style.

Jewellery was to become important for Chanel once again. Her collaboration on this with Robert Goossens bore extraordinarily beautiful fruit, with Byzantine-style brooches and necklaces of green, red, pearl and gold. Their rough-hewn quality complemented the modern aspect of the clothes perfectly; this *faux* intensity aroused the senses and the diamond creations gave the clothes a heightened glamour for evening.

Gabrielle did, of course, succeed magnificently in her mission to lure women's imaginations away from the dictates of Madison Avenue editors and into wearable fashion. The suit would gradually escalate into cardigan form and the lace evening dress continue to evolve to its high point in the late 1950s so that, by the next decade, Chanel could do no wrong.

An article in the New York *Times* days before the 1954 shows stated: 'These days Mademoiselle Chanel is no longer interested in dressing a few hundred private clients. "I will dress thousands of women. I will start with a collection, the same size collection I used to make. About one hundred things, because I must start this way. It won't be a revolution, it won't be shocking. Changes must not be brutal, must not be made all of a sudden. The eye must be given time to adjust itself to a new thought. It will be a collection made by a woman with love."'

Henry CLARKE

RIGHT *The extraordinary pink nylon layer dress.* Life *magazine said Chanel loved the fact that it washes, which sounds an uncharacteristic concern for Mademoiselle.*

OPPOSITE *The ultimate – rose red wool jersey wrapover dress, for late day. Versions from 1916 and 1998 have a similarly dynamic feel for the times.*

Paul HIMMEL

Henry CLARKE

Henry CLARKE

RIGHT *A typical Chanel device – tension between construction and texture – taken to the limit. Bubbly nylon seersucker in bright navy blue plus blown roses worn with the pearl and ruby* sautoir *or long necklace.*

OPPOSITE *The trophy of the 1954 Comeback collection, the demure navy suit and boater in wool jersey.*

Paul HIMMEL

RIGHT *White on white – oversized fleecy coat with huge buttons and buckles, over a knitted thick-rib dress with navy grosgrain detail and theatrical rubies and pearls, the key costume jewels of the collection.*

OPPOSITE *Wool jersey and fur trim – a powerful balance of usefulness and luxury.*

Henry CLARKE

Henry CLARKE

Henry CLARKE

Henry CLARKE

OPPOSITE *Pink ribbons over creamy pintucked gauze, off the shoulder with volumes of shin length skirt – the now-familiar effect of understated grandeur, with no jewellery.*

LEFT *Update on the ballgown, a more assured, womanly shape, with a spontaneous feel, despite the rich fabric (bud-pink Celanese acetate satin, with ruched detail).*

Darling of the fashion world

...1964

Henri CARTIER-BRESSON

'More than ever, US fashion is on Chanel's wavelength; now it's Chanel right down the line – from the top of the head (rounded, bowed, bangs) to the tips of the fingers (in a short glove – her long narrow 18th-century sleeve has made the one-button glove as right as rain again) to the toes (soft and dark surrounded by a sling of really naked-looking kidskin; stockings of the same pinky beige). All deliriously pretty and sexy with one of those brawny Chanel tweeds ... Very correct hang to the jacket, short skirt with a cloche-like slide over hip, lots of action at the hem – couldn't be better.'

VOGUE, FEBRUARY 1ST, 1964

By the time this collection was shown, Chanel had become the darling of the press and fashion cognoscenti. Her suits, particularly from the 1958/59 collection on, were eagerly received. Real women could wear them; those who could not afford to wear them used them for inspiration. For many designers that might be considered unproductive and undesirable, but not so for Coco Chanel. Balenciaga liked to tell a story about how Chanel wore the same suit for a whole weekend house party. Not content with that, she bragged that it was two seasons old. To Chanel, this longevity was the purpose of couture.

For her new 1964 collection, Chanel produced an exact copy of a suit that she had designed for herself two years before. 'The boxy cardigan jacket is a soft beige tweed trimmed with bright red and dark blue braid. The four patch pockets are really pockets and she uses them like purses. The skirt of the same tweed is slim, short and tactically tailored for walking, sitting or anything. With a red or blue matching blouse and her eternal Breton sailor hat, Chanel wears it at lunch, wears it at dinner, wears it at work. No one models a Chanel suit better,' stated the New York *Times*.

For the 1964 collection, the Chanel suit became even more youthful. Although many of the skirts are cut on the knee, and never above it, her suits had a youthful freshness throughout the 60s, largely due to the box pleats or the width of the skirt. Chanel never countenanced shorter skirts, stating that it was 'an exhibition of meat'.

Her suit shapes became a staple of maintstream American sportswear. One event that put Chanel in the history books was the John F. Kennedy assassination in 1963. Jackie Kennedy was wearing a pink Chanel suit with a pillbox hat in the motorcade. This youthful presidency had come to symbolise everything chic and modern.

Some 1964 ensembles reveal Italian an influence in the use of thick knits in undyed wool and strong, 'rustic' shapes; psychedelic and Baroque fabrics were made into neat dresses and coats in lurid colour combinations.

When examining clothes from this collection, it becomes clear what haute couture was all about in the mid-1960s. The chain weights on the jackets, the sleeves and the details of how the dresses or suits fasten show how the suits afford great comfort, despite appearances to the contrary.

As always with Chanel, the suits are superbly cut. Each turnback on a cuff is precise, each sleeve has an attitude of sophistication and each hidden button sits neatly in place. Sleeveless dresses often had a matching cuff on the accompanying jacket. Sometimes a jacket possessed a secondary cuff and cufflink in the 'shirt' fabric to give the illusion of a sleeve. Jackets were lined with matching shirt material and as much effort went into the linings and seams as the outside of the garment. In a couple of years, this sort of finish would become anachronistic and youth fashion would determine that quantity must overtake quality.

At this stage, Chanel clothes looked as youthful as any appearing in the top magazines, yet they were not that different from what Chanel had produced at the beginning of her career. The black sequinned trouser suit, an updated version of the 30s design that had been worn by Diana Vreeland, was universally copied by the young and chic. With its white shirt and cardigan jacket, it was copied in navy by Wallis, an English firm who specialised in emancipating catwalk ideas to suit the student pocketbook. Wallis launched a whole collection based on this season at Chanel.

The real collection, photographed by Henry Clarke for *Vogue*, showed how perfectly Chanel emphasised the vulnerability and youth of women, cutting suits with smaller than average shoulders and a high armhole to produce a longer neck and narrower shoulders. The slightly A-line skirts, cut on the bias in sections for ease of movement, were quite a departure for Chanel, whose typical shape had been narrower the previous season. Here, she let the jackets swing out a tiny amount and emphasised this shape with edging and buttons. This slightly flared-out shape of jacket and skirt stayed with Chanel for some time, even becoming more exaggerated in the 1967/68 collection.

As in previous collections, jacket linings usually matched the blouse fabric to complete the streamlined look; even when the skirt and blouse are in reality a dress, the lining helps to maintain a sense of cohesion in the outfit. The handstitching and tucks around the shoulders help with ease of movement. As always, jackets were weighted with a gold chain in order to create perfect lines.

Buttons were a major part of the look. Gold buttons, cufflinks, even ear buckles and pendants that hung from chain belts all carried the ciphers and symbols beloved by Chanel; lions' heads, interlocking Cs, the number 5, clover, wheat and thistles all make their appearances.

In this collection, 'half daisies' of pearls set in gold were used to adorn

the ears, adding to the youthful image; hair ribbons and ponytails exaggerated that vital schoolgirl feel. Some of Chanel's designs from this period resemble short school pinafore tunics, superbly made in sophisticated colours and fabrics.

The marl tweed coat dress and the suit featured in *Harper's Bazaar* are in muted lilac and raspberry colours, with unusual but subtle undertones of burnt orange and mustard. The lilac suit in the Victoria & Albert Museum in London is intricately made. The blouse and jacket trim feature a large orchid print and the details of the cufflinks, buttons and chains give the outfit maximum effect with very little adornment, as in the 1920s.

Like the suits of the 30s that looked austere, the cream cowl-necked dress and coat dress are in fact cunningly and beautifully constructed to look very flattering when worn. The coat dress has a big round neck trimmed in 'pulled' bouclé wool, while the body is in large looseweave squares of the same colour and weight. The front of the coat buttons to one side with two bold, square buttons. The dress (not to be worn with it) has a heavy, narrow roll neck, a blind front opening and a tie-belt with side panels attached. It zips from the waist down and the wrists have tag cuffs. It is modern and sophisticated, with harmonious dimensions.

There are, of course, lots of black suits in the collection. One of the most spectacular is unfitted at the back; another has black frogging and a green-and-white raw silk 'shirt'. One of the most popular among them is also the plainest. It has a boxy jacket and is unformed at the back with lots of small pockets with sculptural chevron detail and a gardenia. The white underblouse is piqué.

The blue suit with the bright pink, blue and metallic gold 'blouse' is an extreme take on the usual Chanel suit, its informality conveyed by checks and a scarf. There is also a white bouclé suit with double-edged braid and matching pockets, and a tweed coat dress, unfitted and long-sleeved.

The coats in the collection are short, fitted and trimmed with fur. Romy Schneider was pictured wearing one in *Paris Match*, and the whole outerwear collection was pictured in the boutique at rue Cambon among huge mirrors and bottles of Chanel No 5.

For evening wear, there were suits made in jazzy patterns and outré colours. Again, Chanel used the day-suit shape and used the fabric to denote the evening suit's formality. The Countess of Manchester's black

HATAMI

HATAMI

OPPOSITE *The Chanel suit, little adornment except 2 gilt chains, hallmark buttons and the trademark slingbacks give the right length of leg. Photographed in Mademoiselle's apartment.*

LEFT *Always the clever contradiction – formal day costume in dressed-down stripes.*

RIGHT *The all time classic cardigan suit, with grosgrain bow, pearls and gilt chain belt.*

OPPOSITE *The youthful shape of the 60s suit; schoolgirl bow, camellia and blend of tweed and checks.*

HATAMI

Henry CLARKE

HATAMI

OPPOSITE *60s brocade catsuit with sheerest black coat. Chanel loved to undercut dramatic fabrics with younger styles.*

LEFT *'Matelassé' white suit, gilt buttons, saucer hat and camellias – this very popular theme recurs under the design direction of Karl Lagerfeld in the 80s.*

Henry CLARKE

RIGHT *Equal parts coquetry and frosty protocol – diagonal cut checks and flowers, lined in textured silk.*

OPPOSITE *These bulkier tweeds in raspberry and mustard feature a shorter jacket with double flap pockets, reveres and turn-back cuffs emphasising the longer, leaner skirt. New-style hammered gilt chains and matching hat complete the new classic look.*

Richard DORMER

HATAMI

OPPOSITE *The slimline cut fur-trimmed wool coats were the bestsellers of the 1963/64 collection.*

LEFT *Chanel's eternal favourite idea – this incarnation of the trousersuit was the most influential.*

HATAMI

The first ready to wear collection

...1978

Tony KENT

To many people today, Couture means a special fit of jeans or a hideously avant-garde notion, to promote an image de marque that benefits from the filtering down of its impact in order to sell tights or nail polish.

In the hey day of Chanel, right up to the 1970s, Couture meant quality, the artistry, a one-to-one relationship, one of the most intimate and trusting. To have the great Gabrielle Chanel fit one of her creations with your shape in mind, must have been the ultimate fashion fantasy; the way she fitted the clothes on the body and her innate instinct for how to make the figure look its absolute best, even if it took hours.

Chanel's 1971 collection, the one just before she died, was well received. It marked a renaissance in knitwear and twinsets, and featured strongly the thin whipcord belts that she had originally devised in the late 1920s. Due to the success of the film *Bonnie and Clyde* and other retro movies that were released during the late 60s and early 70s, women at all levels of the fashion pyramid were keen to sport the styles of the Jazz Age.

The black chiffon evening dress that she designed for the 1971 collection, with its huge pompom sleeves and its long, flaring skirt, shows many influences from the 1937–39 collections and the refined, clipped romanticism at which she was so expert. A dress designed by Karl Lagerfeld for the 1983 collections bears similarities.

Since the 70s was possibly the most innovative and varied decade in 20th century fashion, drawing as heavily as it did on the late 30s and 40s for inspiration, one can only wonder what Chanel herself would have created at this time had she lived.

During the 40s themselves, she was in retirement. The short period from around 1937 to the outbreak of World War II give only a small glimpse of her design ideas during this time. Given that Chanel vehemently disliked the fussiness of the post-war New Look, it would be interesting to know what she would have thought of the fashions of the 1970s, when so many of her themes were re-worked – clothing for the working woman, the trouser suit, halter necks and the new Edwardian look that proliferated throughout the 70s were all avenues that Chanel had explored 40 years before.

After Chanel's death in 1971, the House of Chanel faced decline. There was a frustrating double-edged sword to wield if Chanel's legacy was to continue, due to the necessity of blending tradition with innovation. The genius of Chanel was no longer there to bend the rules and thus caution reigned in the House of Chanel.

Meanwhile, the experimentation of the youth market had caused a decline in the world of couture as a whole. The word 'boutique' sadly now meant a place where quirky little numbers were run up overnight by a novice, with the idea behind the garment being more important than for how long it would stay sewn together. Political attitudes were hardening to the left and privilege had seemingly had its day. There was a crisis in the whole couture business, as the best-dressed lists strayed into jeans and T-shirt territory. For Chanel, without Mademoiselle, there was a tightrope ahead that had to be crossed with each collection. How could they stay true to the ideals of the Chanel of the past and be innovative at the same time? How could they serve the clients of the past and lure new ones away from the high street 'groovy' shops now frequented by most women?

Tales of how Chanel would rip up a sleeve, keep models standing for hours at a time, bark at them as they wilted beneath her indefatigable gaze, and fit garments to perfection on the body to show exactly where the seat was without making a show of it were legion. To many, that was the meaning of couture but it now only seemed to matter to a few friends. The world of couture was at its nadir and there were no easy answers for anyone.

By 1978, Ready to Wear had been deemed to be the only sensible avenue to take, and the company started to rethink matters. In 1977 Philippe Guibourgé was appointed to produce Chanel's first Ready to Wear collection. Jersey was reintroduced as the desireable fabric – fitting was not deemed necessary, since its shape would adapt, and it had the right combination of informal easy shape and 'dressed up' elements to suit the times. Gabrielle Chanel did not choose a successor so it is difficult to know how she saw the future of the house. During this time scent and perfume were hugely successful and led the way in the commercial market.

The cardigan had been such a key element in the Chanel style that it was entirely natural that the cardigan suit shape of the late 50s and early 60s should be adapted to the straighter, less cluttered format of the late 70s, with its understated Sloane or BCBG accessories and sensible shoes. It was the perfect medium between dressing in a suit and wearing a T-shirt.

The 1978 collection's navy suit was the perfect uniform for women who wished to appear smart and unfussy. It was ideal for both married women of a certain age and for working women who wished to appear fashionable but serious. The suits were quite successful at adapting the image of the Chanel suit to complement the mood of the times and were accessible to more people.

There was a whole new generation of women who were not being catered for by the couture industry, including those who did not seek couture because of political ideals against elitism or because they favoured the street credibility of wearing younger styles. It was impossible for Chanel and its competitors to try to compete in the arena of sportswear and dance

Tight black top and mid-calf tulle skirt trimmed with ribbons has the contemporary feel of the dance craze and the delicacy of the haute-couture design repertoire

styles, which were becoming popular in the 70s. The leotard and layered ballet skirt outfit from the 1978 collection looks very attractive and is undoubtedly well-made, but the fickle market of the time probably wanted 'the real thing', from dance shops.

The renewed interest in couture in general was very shortly about to happen but, in the meantime, there was someone who was very much in tune with the spirit of the time and who was true to the ideals of Mademoiselle Chanel, so much so that Chanel herself loved to refer to him as her heir apparent. 'The more he is like me, the more I like him,' she frequently used to say of the young Yves St Laurent. He was the keeper of the flame of the trouser suit, which he was to reinvent over and over again in various guises: safari, caftan and trousers, and the colossally successful tuxedo.

The idea behind this grown-up trouser suit was that the more spare and tailored it was, the more it made a woman look feminine. Not the two-piece with trainers and a push-up bra of the 90s, not the discreet femininity of Armani suits, but the woman who is grown up and able to handle her femaleness. That was what Chanel and Marlene Dietrich had in common when they had explored the man/woman boundary back in the 20s and 30s, delving into the power and the mystery of androgyny.

Classic, masculine lines with a very well-toned but feminine body shape underneath has become the byword for sophistication and sexuality. The child-woman has come and gone, but Chanel and Yves St Laurent have always stood alone and almost beyond fashion with their concept of timeless fashion to suit women of any age.

Chanel was always looking for ways to make women feel youthful but age was for the most part irrelevant to her and the wearers of her clothes. St Laurent does the same; it is always the wearer who brings something to the look, and the wearer should always be the centre of attention rather than the clothes themselves.

Both of these designers have been tremendously successful in creating exciting gender ambivalence. In the 90s, crossing the gender barrier is still the ultimate statement of allure and power. When Chanel first raided the gentleman's dressing room, it had a major impact on the form of women's clothing and bodies, and affected how a woman felt about her sexuality. Little has changed today.

For the Ready to Wear collection in 1978, Chanel's little black dress had turned into something more dressed

up, with a tiny white peter pan collar on a dipped neckline, a neat if longer black bow and a flared skirt in chiffon. Worn with high slingback shoes decorated with pompoms, it shows how the fantasy Hollywood feeling of Anthony Price and Thierry Mugler was coming face to face with the Edwardian look and resolving their immense differences. The offspring of this cross-pollination was the power-dressing fashion of the 1980s, with its masculine wide shoulders and female body-consciousness everywhere else.

Retro was expressed in knitwear and jackets; only St Laurent and the American market revisited Chanel's resortwear influences, with wide white trousers and backless tops worn with huge sunhats, espadrilles, bangles, baubles and lots of beads. Around this time, Karl Lagerfeld, already a prolific and prodigious talent, was investigating some of the familiar themes he would later use for Chanel – long, lean skirts with white shirts and tank tops, huge brassy cuff bracelets and black-and-white suits. The incredibly romantic evening dresses he designed for Chloe feature layers of silk and lace and were worn with strong, one colour sashes and high satin shoes.

In 1954 Lagerfeld and St Laurent had won joint first in a prestigious fashion award in Paris that would launch the career of each one. The two men were never similar, but one of them, Yves Saint Laurent had all the hallmarks of the great Gabrielle Chanel and the other, Lagerfeld has become the supreme translator of her thoughts for our times, as well as producing as many as 19 collections a year and his other projects. His great strength, particularly at Chanel, is that although he is clearly gifted, his style is flexible and not associated with one look. Others had already tried their hand at the Chanel style, the *Premiers d'ateliers* Mr Jean and Mrs Yvonne from 1973 to 1983. However, it seemed that no one could make sense of the current climate.

Fashion for the most part then was divided into a bulky, baggy shape and a sylph-like silhouette. The head was ideally small and neat, with low pony-tails caught in Chanel-esque bows, or hair left long, straight and loose. The slingback shoe was compatible with almost everything at this stage, except the dirndl skirts and anoraks of the more 'way out' designers. Chanel was infrequently mentioned in fashion reports from the shows at this time. However, it must be said that many of the success stories of the period are long-forgotten, while Chanel lives on and continues to evolve.

Henry CLARKE

Mike REINHARDT

OPPOSITE *A more relaxed, squarely cut suit with white shirt and large contrast bow-tie.*

LEFT *Open-knit schoolgirl jersey and flared skirt with bright, white knitted tie and gilt and pearl jewellery.*

Jean-Pierre LEDOS

OPPOSITE *The little black dress 78 style; white collar, ribbon bow and cinch waist belt with bejewelled clasp and showgirl shoes.*

LEFT *Barely-there see-through chiffon drapery for theatrical night wear and gold evening slingbacks.*

OVERLEAF LEFT *Shirred silky knit ensemble with cinch belt, drama courtesy of clasp belt and contrast cardigan with braided trim left and the mannish tweed, heavy belt and panama feminised by velvet trim, and a wide expanse of leg.*

OVERLEAF RIGHT *Demurely black and white – the dimensions of the Chanel suit have been altered to the new wide-shouldered, unconstructed shape of the late 70s and early 80s.*

Mike REINHARDT

Mike REINHARDT

Rococo Chanel

...1983

Chris MOORE

'It was high noon, haute chic and a high point in the fashion calendar of Paris. The gilt chairs lined up in Chanel's first floor salon in a narrow street behind the Ritz were labelled Pompidou, Adjani, Rothschild ....' Liz Smith for *London Evening Standard*, 26 Jan 1983.

When Karl Lagerfeld unveiled his first collection for the House of Chanel, in 1983, there was a familiar feeling of controversy about the styles emerging which had not occurred since the days of Chanel herself. As Anne Price of *Country Life* put it 'the big problem was how to adapt a legend without destroying it, when the legend was too useful and too popular to kill.' Lagerfeld had the reputation at the time of being rather outré. As a boy, he had attended Chanel's 1954 comeback show with his mother.

In many ways, that collection and this one had much in common, in that the customers decided on its success before the press. As in 1954, the customers who bought Chanel from 1983 onwards were from a broader age range and even wider spectrum of society than had previously been seen, not to mention those admiring onlookers, who saw the point of the collection but couldn't afford the real thing.

Nina Hyde wrote of the collection: 'A lot of people have been concerned that Lagerfeld means the end of Chanel, but the house is too smart to throw out the suit. It works and Karl is likely to continue with it ... It doesn't look like what he does for Fendi or Chloe, but it's his alright.' Actually, even though part of it was his, he had also collaborated with others on the prêt-à-porter collection.

The triumph of the 1983 collection was for many people the trompe l'oeil dress, with embroidery by Lesage. It puns on Mademoiselle's penchant for piling on the jewellery, real and fake and is reminiscent of her own trompe l'oeil dress in the 20s. There is even a 'pretend' necklace at the back, mounted on the neckline of the dress, while the back is bare. The traditional motifs of Chanel's favourite belt with clover and pearls, pearls and more pearls are there. Even the wrists are laden with 'jewellery' in her typical combinations of 'pearl,' 'pigeon blood rubies,' 'gold' and 'deepest emerald,' like a Maharajah's jewel casket. The perfectly simple long sleeved, straight cut dress in black silk crepe hangs like a dream and is represented in the collection at the Metropolitan Museum in New York and also in the personal collection of the fashion collector and commentator Tina Chow.

Lagerfeld diplomatically said: 'A very static image has emerged based on Chanel's last years, so I've looked over her whole career and found something much more interesting.' He drew inspiration from her work of the 20s and 30s and ignored her 50s Comeback designs, when hemlines were frozen just below the knee. Lagerfeld asserted that Chanel used hundreds of different skirt lengths. The following season, Lagerfeld used the ideas and inspiration again for his long and short white silk suits.

Marie-Hélène de Rothschild, who possibly knew better than anyone, said of Lagerfeld's designs: 'He's got a feeling for Chanel, but it's not yet complete. Someone has to tell him more about her. She had such perfect proportions. But no one could have done it on the first try. It will come.'

In the event, Lagerfeld's creations proved to be the new look that women clamoured for. The suits were in the main long-line with either stitched-down pleats or a windmill skirt, which was constructed from four panels that moved aside to gracefully emphasise the stride. Others were shorter and tighter, which became the byword for 80s and early 90s fashion.

Underneath, Lagerfeld placed vests and shell blouses in white ottoman and piqué. He liberated tweeds from the restrictive palette of soft pastels in flat fabrics and once again showed the multi-colour checks in slightly off-beat combinations.

Accessories were both plentiful as well as eclectic, as Mademoiselle had herself advocated in the 1920s. Pearls and gold chains predominated, wound around the hips and waist, together with huge faux gems, bracelets and chain belts of interlocking Cs.

Rhinestones were evident almost everywhere in accessories – belts, necklaces, bracelets, earrings and slick black ribbon headbands. Large, romantic bows appeared on boaters; saucer brims and hats also appeared as tweed fedoras.

The interlocking C motifs were to be seen on everything – from the famous court-shoe heels to the handbags and the chunky ropes of the gilt jewellery. Buttons again featured Mademoiselle's beloved and well-known ciphers.

The dressier evening wear was Karl Lagerfeld's strongest selection, and featured Mademoiselle's preferred colours of red, white, blue and black. The very simple shape of a black silk or mousseline tank-top dress with or without frills proved very popular.

Lagerfeld also used a lot of elegant, beaded brocades and baguette beads to give emphasis, shape and definition to the upper body. This work saw the start of an historic link between the prestigious House of Chanel and the ultra-respectable company Lesage.

Pyjamas, greatly favoured evening wear items for Mademoiselle, were a triumph at this show, in the form of a white satin jacket, worn over satin trousers, which, according to *Country Life* journalist Anne Price: 'looks as wicked in 1983 as it did decades ago.'

They also remade the 1950s black jacket over a panel skirt in navy blue wool, with the typical chain belt and camelia. The smart navy jacket over a white silk shell blouse with matching revers on the jacket, the white broad-brimmed boater and the mid-calf skirt are all redolent of both the 1950s Chanel suit and the earlier suits from the 1937 collections.

Cardigans were used for both day and evening wear to great effect. The cardigan being such an important element in the Chanel repertoire, was astutely featured as both slouchy and sporty for day and long, simple and elegant over plain black evening dresses for night.

The black silk chiffon dress with camisole and circular skirt was not legitimately 'Chanel', but the concept of putting white and gold beads on the bodice and hip, with the black

Chris MOORE

suede belt with its 'fence' of diamanté Cs, is absolutely true to form.

In the asymmetric Solstiss guipure lace dress with its contrasting diaphanous black waves of tulle – from Babouin – beneath the hip, Lagerfeld is again mining the rich seam of Chanel of the late 30s. The front is cut just like a swimsuit and the back plunges down, highlighting that vital interface that Chanel herself used between formality and casualness. The emphasis on the hip is a key Chanel element. Gloves are an extra reminder of 30s glamour.

The long, square-necked, evening dress in silk tulle from Hurel with its exaggerated pompom sleeves is a young woman's dress. The pompoms are echoed around the hips. The band around the low neckline adds a rare combination of weight and lightness just where they are needed.

With the day suits, it was hard to get the balance right between the freedom necessary for a ready to wear suit and the perfectionism demanded by the Chanel shape, which was essentially a small armhole. The solution was to make the armhole slightly larger and lower, so that it would be comfortable.

The navy tweed suit, with military double-breasted jacket and cut-out front, shows how the tailoring of the 80s body-hugging form and the traditional principles of Chanel style were reconciled. The longer, slimmer skirts are more Chanel, since they have the narrow hip shape that she was known for. For the following season, the armholes were cut smaller and the suits shaped rather more as we have come to expect of the Chanel style rather than being based on the 'Faubourg St Honoré-style homage to Chanel' that Lagerfeld tried to create. It seemed hard for people to understand that Karl Lagerfeld was not hired by the House of Chanel in order to 'be Chanel', although, superstitiously, he kept the sign saying Mademoiselle Chanel on the door. Rather, he was employed to make the Chanel image work for the present and the future.

The collection for Spring/Summer was more even-handed, with added emphasis on the 50s influences of the Chanel formula. With opportunities for balancing light and dark with the Spring/Summer colours and lighter, more supple fabrics, Chanel's easy wearability and easiness on the eye was once again the most recognisable story in town.

The black velvet evening dress that buttons down the side, with a flouncy sailor collar edged in white ermine, is nearer the mark. It has that blend of informality of shape and stateliness of

HORST

fabric at which Chanel herself was so brilliant. The chain belt accentuates narrowness of hip and the skirt flares out in pleats below.

Even the least likely combinations, such as the haltered lace dress with tulle fishtail, tulle-frilled hips and tulle-frilled sleeves, have the power to conjure up the elements of Chanel in the 20s and 30s without being pure homage. The diamanté jewellery with pearls and the No 5 diamanté bracelet add the raciness lacking in some of the other experiments.

The jackets with oversized collars, the hobble-inducing skirts and the slightly A-line tweeds are unmemorable today and look slightly dated. For Chanel, the fit was all and it was absolutely fundamental to creating clothes with a youthful feeling, despite her favoured longer skirt lengths and disciplined approach to clothes.

The dress and cardigan with their bugle beaded bands and interlocking C motif at the waist and the wool-crepe trouser suit with its sailor trousers featuring brass buttons are pure Chanel in spirit. The jacket has a single row of brass buttons; the heavy silk grosgrain short-sleeved shirt has a black silk bow tie and buttons onto the trousers. A black ribboned straw boater goes with it and, when worn with a long row of beads, it revives the issue of androgyny.

The jewellery that was used during the shows was created by Gripoix and Ugo Camerana, and was one of the principle style determinators. The abundance of 'junk' jewellery and the dark clothes relieved at key areas by sparkle and pearls was what made the collection work for Chanel.

As if there were a need for proof of the success of this collection, Chanel copies began to spring up everywhere, including *Harpers & Queen*, which featured several Chanel pieces in one issue, together with the chance for readers to buy Chanel-style palazzo pants. *Tatler* focused on the separates from the prêt-à-porter collection and a little black dress with white collar, cuffs and bow tie; 80s magazines would never be without at least several Chanel numbers from then on.

Chanel was as popular as it had ever been. No one could have predicted the renewed success or what riotous interpretations would come into being. The important thing was that, once again, the House of Chanel had triumphed over the runway-edge 'experts'; a lost generation of clients was reclaimed and an ever-multiplying world of devotees would be clamouring for the latest ideas from the best established fashion house in Paris.

RIGHT *All woman – this dress is all about silhouette and suggestion with hourglass curves and sensuous beaded evening gloves.*

OPPOSITE *The new Garçonne – breton hat, sailor trousers with monogrammed gilt buttons either side and a long rope of beads for that essential ambiguity.*

Bruce WEBER

Bruce WEBER

ROCOCO CHANEL / 1983

RIGHT *Pompom sleeves and ruffles on a body-hugging form with accent of white at decollete' and important bow jewellery in diamonds and pearls. This look might be reminiscent of the dresses Chanel herself wore on stage.*

OPPOSITE *White asymmetric-cut guipure lace dress and finest black filmy tulle stole for complete contrast and theatricality.*

Bruce WEBER

ROCOCO CHANEL / 1983

HORST

HORST

OPPOSITE *This curvaceous double-breasted jacket with padded shoulders and matching svelte long-line skirt show the evolution of the Chanel suit.*

LEFT *Karl Lagerfeld used many different sources of ideas from Mademoiselle Chanel's past creations, here the influences of the 50s are clearly recognisable.*

HORST

132 ROCOCO CHANEL / 1983

LEFT *Richly encrusted embroidery with a perfectly plain silk skirt. You only get this shape in* Haute *Haute Couture .*

Street couture

1993

Ten years on from his debut, working from Mademoiselle's own atelier in rue Cambon, Karl Lagerfeld had a free hand. His assured idea of his role in the House of Chanel, coupled with a shrewd knowledge of his audience, led him to make some outrageous statements on the runway. The supermodel cult greatly added to this and, when Naomi, Claudia and Linda were spotted in their own time with the interlocking Cs motif on everything from buttons and bags to trainers and rucksacks, it seemed that nothing was too ignominious to be endowed with these fashion power statements.

The little black dress was updated once again and became, irrevocably, every woman's secret weapon. It was taken apart and given elongated, sinuous new dimensions. It was intended to be worn with the highest of heels and elaborate jewellery.

All of the original Chanel elements were big and fiercely ostentatious. The chains, pearls and accessories had become massive and easily outshone everything else that appeared in the collection, but they were instantly recognisable to the world as the very signature features invented by the great Gabrielle Chanel herself.

For the previous collection, Karl Lagerfeld had linked the chains to the world of rappers, most of whom now wore their wealth hung around their necks like an alternative currency. He had also made a connection with the world of bikers and heavy metal by teaming chains with leather jackets and biker caps, which were worn over ballgowns in pastel shades of silk tulle and with high, spiked heels.

These shock tactics paid off very handsomely, since this style of 'in your face' bravura, with its surrealistic connotations and subtext about street fashion, was just the ticket for the high-octane, self-referential image-making that was rampant in this age of conspicuous consumption.

So much more money was now in circulation and the items that people bought had to stand for something so much more than they ever had before. Now women wanted both tradition and innovation, and an attitude of confidence and figure-hugging, daring glamour. Chanel had all that in abundance. Although the collection was often criticised by the cognoscenti as being closer in spirit to Chanel's arch enemy Elsa Schiaparelli, women could not get enough of these abbreviated versions of the Chanel suit and oversized accessories, paying homage to the heritage of Gabrielle's ideas with the wit and jargon of the contemporary world thrown in.

The colour palette of the tweeds and woollens was more strident than anything that had ever appeared in the original Chanel colour spectrum. The tweeds had undergone radical changes since the days of the old regime; not only were they produced in fuschia, mustard and scarlet combinations, but were also considerably shorter and pounds lighter in weight.

The midriff was now bare and the Lagerfeld tweeds bore absolutely no resemblance to traditional Scottish tweed. From 1991 onwards, the black skirts worn with white shirts and low-slung chain belts were inspired more by the sassy, savvy working girl than by the charmed life of Chanel. As in the 1920s and 1960s, women were enjoying a new fitness boom and another spurt of financial independence, so they were not going to let the rewards of these pursuits vegetate, they wanted to spend their money on clothes and accessories that were as sassy and savvy as themselves.

Women were by now accustomed to the flashier, sexier shape of Chanel clothes. This sexiness was part and parcel of the fashion scene as a whole and meant that any resistance to the changes taking place in the House of Chanel was unnoticeable. A new generation of women had become devotees of Chanel and the old guard, for the most part, were enjoying being helped to look young again.

There were, of course, copies of this new, sexy couture style but, in using street themes as the inspiration for their designs, haute couture houses were able to feed off street fashion while the street copies did not have the cachet of the real thing and were therefore not worth having. Chanel bags were now given exclusive *cartes d'authenticité* and the clothes had serial numbers as proof that they were the real thing.

Gabrielle Chanel had been unable to accept many changes in fashion, but all influences were now relevant. The image of the suit became less formal and the midriff was bared. Leggings and tight trousers worn with loose shirts and black ties signified a move to a complete lack of formality; this sports garb was, in fact, an update on Chanel's original look. In Chanel's early days, the future of fashion had been sportswear; its fortunes had turned full circle and it was now firmly back in the limelight once more. Several big fashion empires launched sportswear lines during this period and the question on every designer's lips was: how formal would fashion ever need to be again?

Ladies who lunched would now be skating to the restaurant and dressing in a way that rendered the need for tailored clothing in the daytime defunct, entreated Lagerfeld. On the street, Chanel jackets were being worn with ripped jeans and cowboy boots, so was it not indeed more valid to start at that end and work on from there? These informal ensembles were heavily dependent on accessories, for without them this would just be another youth look. However, with the chain belt, bag and huge emblematic earrings, overseen by Victoire de Castellane, it was something special. It was so hip it hurt.

Chris MOORE

The accessories were all highly exaggerated in form. The chain bags were given a makeover in the colour department but, even in the regulation navy version, there had been many variations since the late 1980s. They appeared in French or Italian leather, quilted or with Cs sewn into the actual bag. Both small and huge versions of the bag were available in myriad fabrics, beading and shapes. For all occasions and each season some new twist was sure to appear, so that women could not resist buying just one more.

The shoe permutations were also legion: deck shoes, platforms, evening court shoes that were so elegant it was almost unbearable to wear them in case they became damaged, ballerina pumps – the staple of the summer months – as well as a huge range of lace-ups, loafers and boots.

The Mademoiselle watch made its first appearance in 1990. This lovely, square-faced watch, with a strap of five rows of pearls, was advertised in the world's choice fashion magazines for several years and quickly became a 'must-have' item. Pearls themselves were a very sentimental item for Chanel and they were now put to use to help transform the watch from a functional item into a piece of jewellery. After almost a decade of seeing the Rolex as the cognoscenti's watch of choice, it was now time for Chanel to enter this market. Even casual clothes could be dressed up with Chanel's beautiful timepiece, not just evening wear.

The matelassé leather bags were just the right side of the 'tough girl' image and, just as Chanel had once coaxed her clients into sweaters inspired by Parisian street gangs, Karl Lagerfeld was putting supermodels into these esoteric slouch ensembles. The message seemed to be: if you have to ask ... don't bother.

The merchandising strategies for Chanel products had now changed in the world of Ready to Wear. Led by catwalk overstatement, the designs were then translated into purchases that would suit buyers at each end of the spectrum, from those who could afford to drape themselves in Chanel from tip to toe, to those whose goal purchase was a single chain bag or pair of earrings from one of 40 Chanel boutiques around the world. When Lagerfeld started, there were just nine boutiques. The world of fashion had become extremely pressurised and competitive during this period, largely due to an extraordinary media awareness and the explosion of fashion images in all formats.

Camellia brooches and scarves, ear buckles, bows, rows of outsized pearls and brooches in red and green stones all made their appearances in the 93 collection, as well as sunglasses festooned with Cs on a bed of quilting.

For evening wear, the collection did a complete volte-face from its themes for daywear and produced an ultra-romantic look, including Hurel black mousseline dresses and *belle époque* hats by Philip Treacy, bustier dresses and camellia brooches, atavistic crucifixes with huge Byzantine stones, trouser suits with bolero jackets and plunge necklines, evening dresses with brass buttons and white collar and tie.

The eternal man/woman gender issue of Chanel was complemented by Gabrielle's original ideas of informal daywear and exciting evening wear. The colours that predominated in the 93 collection were more intense than ever before, although there was still lots of black, but the inspiration was perhaps more Roman or Middle Ages than 20s Paris or London. These dresses were minimal, draped and some had heavy chains and huge flower medallions on the tiny bodices.

A tiny halter-necked dress with a mousseline bustier shows how much the bare minimum held up by a collar and chain and worn with ankle boots can startle the onlooker. Another tiny dress of pearly tulle with a long train and separate arms has invented a new standard for Chanel. The dresses were fluid, draped or see-through but always decorated and sometimes with a train. Black was promoted to decorative uses and featured in plumes, embroidery and sequins; red and nude were seen, too.

The trenchcoat was brought back from oblivion, where it had been languishing despite being singularly important for Mademoiselle Chanel. This time it sported sashes and bows and the sleeves were elevated in status with unusual shapes.

When the suit was seen, it was shapely and short, worn with the indispensable two-tone, high-heeled court shoes and a broad-brimmed straw hat on the back of the head. When worn with gloves, it was seen to be quite dressed up enough for those who had the figure for it. Who needed a skirt or trousers? If they did want pants, there was only one pair of them in this collection; legs were to be seen and not hidden. The collection's look was purely and simply feminine, with empire dresses for evening, lots of drapery and embroidered coat dresses. This collection was full of surprises on the long-understood lines of Chanel's principles.

Chris MOORE

Chris MOORE

Chris MOORE

OPPOSITE *The briefest, most detailed mermaid suit in the world, with matching gauntlets and gold sequin trimmed stole and sparkle-encrusted hair jewellery.*

LEFT *The crumbly-textured tweeds are frayed and minimised to almost swimsuit size suits to most uplifting effect.*

Chris MOORE

Chris MOORE

OPPOSITE *Labels and logos on the most unassuming items, although the camellia, chain belt and tweeds are all given an outing.*

LEFT *Influences of the late 30s find their way in; the turban, the sports dress worn over long white drill skirt. Charm bracelet completes the allusion.*

BELOW LEFT *The witty play on the Chanel style elements are made into a winning fabric for beach-wear.*

Chris MOORE

OPPOSITE *Classic Chanel – the ever-green combination of diaphonous black on white, frou-frou hem, strategically-placed embroidery and wristlets pay homage to Chanel's early music hall career.*

OPPOSITE *The outsize cross necklaces from this collection, teamed with palest, most revealing gowns recall Gabrielle Chanel's large Byzantine crosses with all manner of outfits in her earlier collections.*

Chris MOORE

Chris MOORE

OPPOSITE *The deep 'V' back, fur cuffs and slim skirt are redolent of the late 30s, whereas the textural contrasts are wildly postmodern.*

LEFT *Outsize accessories feature heavily in this collection, while the little hat is saucily in keeping with Mademoiselle's classics.*

Chris MOORE

Chris MOORE

OPPOSITE *The artful dodger models sportswear – the gilt chains look as though they have been customised by rap artists.*

LEFT *The blazer and the white shirt appear here with the black sweater, the gilt chain and the camellia, although any sense of tradition is turned on its head.*

Chris MOORE

OPPOSITE *The abbreviated jacket with the tightest arms and the gilt chains here could not be more different from previous versions.*

LEFT *The little black dress in its punk permutation, with gypsyish attitude.*

Now and Zen

...1998

Michel EULER

The 1998/99 Autumn/Winter collection was to surprise everyone. Just when people had become used to the strong identity of the Chanel image under the direction of Karl Lagerfeld and his team – the interlocking Cs, the characteristic snappy suits (even with the long skirts of the 1997 haute couture collections, the suits had a ladylike quality with the huge, teetering hats and bare torso under half-done-up, hip-length jackets) – it was still the dressed-up sexiness that one had come to expect from Chanel. None of this could prepare the onlookers at the shows for what Suzy Menkes, the international fashion arbiter from the *Herald Tribune*, christened 'Now and Zen'.

'The latest collections for Chanel indicate the new direction in thought as well as design. The recent collections have been preoccupied by the golden age of couture, as if in some way an explanation must be found for its existence. Chanel paid homage to the 20s, with cardigans, huge ropes of pearls and some stunning evening looks, said to reflect the influence of Amanda Harlech, former muse to Galliano at Dior. However, the mood has quickly turned to look ahead to the new millennium and if any explanation or intellectual argument is in order, then it must be oriented in that direction and answer the question "What is the meaning of *luxe* now and what is 'modern' today?"'

The ideas and ideals of modernity were of supreme importance during the first half of the 20th century, and particularly during the space age, but since post-modernism reached the mass consciousness, retro styles have become a convenient refuge. Many fashion designers repeatedly indulge themselves in a favourite era. Those who are adventurous and forge ahead are frequently seen as formulaic or are allocated a 'cult status'.

For Chanel, the 1998 collection was particularly interesting because of its departure into Deconstruction, its turning towards the East and the conceptual reinvention that it underwent, as witnessed in the daring little twists in details or, more often, lack of them. These clothes are to the 80s suit what Modernism, performance art and 90s architectural innovations are to 80s corporate values, where buyers fought to pay inflated prices for everything from a watch to a Van Gogh. The clothes of this 1998 collection are very provocative and seek to make us question our preconceptions of fashion on the eve of a new dawn.

As we have long come to expect, this charting of unknown territory is not a new experience for the House of Chanel. Karl Lagerfeld himself had moved into a new arena with his art gallery in Paris and his photographic interest in architecture, as evidenced in the pictures he took for the prêt-à-porter collection, which were set in an angular architectural landscape that served to highlight the soft, rounded shapes of the hats and bags and imparted an almost organic sense of proportion to the clothes.

The collection also highlights what Chanel was doing as long ago as 1916, chivvying away at outmoded fashion ideas and unnecessary trappings. More recently, there have been some controversial 'faces of Chanel', including Kirsten McMenemy, Karen

Elson and Erin O'Connor – who wears her hair like a raven-black paintbrush with matching heavy, blackened eyebrows – and this serves to emphasise the house's new departure.

This striking departure from the main themes and signature elements of Chanel, such as buttons and gilt chains, shows how ruthlessly Karl Lagerfeld aims to leave behind the fixation on a golden age of fashion. However, the collection still stays in keeping with Mademoiselle Chanel's love of Eastern philosophy; the riding skirts she favoured in her early life also make their appearance again in the suits of Lagerfeld's 1998 prêt-à-porter collection. The spareness of the clothing provides the ultimate backdrop for the jewellery collections, with some of the haute couture evening dresses taking their influence directly from the jewellery pieces.

The new 2005 bag replaces the 2.55 quilted bag as the accessory for the new age, although, of course, different versions on the original model are still available. This futuristic piece of engineering is designed in accordance with the principles of advanced technology. Weighing about as much as a feather, the bag is ergonomically proportioned to be neither rigid nor soft and to fit all the contours of the body, so that it is as comfortable as a pillow while still being a supremely stylish and very practical accessory.

Inside, eight nylon sections open up like a fan to provide space for all the indispensable items that most women carry around. The removable sanded aluminium strap is quite discreet in its display of the CC logo; the discs at either end are engraved with the logo. The bag's construction echoes the sinuous flexibility of the diamanté jewellery, which features bracelets, belts and necklaces, and the construction of the fine jewellery of Chanel.

Although the 2005 bag's beautiful aerodynamic design is based on the principles of the automobile industry, the streamlined, automated production process used for making cars does not apply to Chanel – more than half the production process for making the 2005 bag is carried out by hand. The rounded shape of the bag is echoed by the collection's half-helmet, half-cloche, hat, which makes a small head that is accentuated by the round collars of the clothes, which are worn off the neck.

The prêt-à-porter collection features novelty at every level. The Paris show was presented in light, white rooms so that the audience could clearly see and appreciate the innovative fabrics, which the New York *Times* called 'a

Chris MOORE

marriage of Japanese textile advances and French luxury'. The more neutral shades of black, beige and off-white contrasted with the autumnal colour themes of plum, brown and greeny-bronze that resonated throughout the collection's tweeds.

The new length of the robin's egg blue and monochrome riding skirts, pocket-detailed sweaters and jersey dresses with draped crossover tops seek to reinvent fashion to create a mood of serenity, fluidity and totally uncontrived, easy elegance. The use of fluffy cream mohair in big wrap coats (similar to a coat dress from the 60s), the white ankle boots with square toes, the white cording on the suits, and the white camellia in the hair and on lapels bring light to dark-season fashion. There are oversized mannish tweed coats, like 20s college letterman's coats, and long cardigans.

For evening wear, there are parma violet, deep purple, charcoal or olive cocktail dresses of the utmost simplicity in thick satin crepe with unlined short mauve or cerise mohair coats for contrast. The pintucked organza dress in black is refined and restrained, yet full in shape. Specially embroidered lace with the name Chanel dancing through it is worked into long sheath dresses, some incredibly low-cut as well as cut away at the sides to reveal diaphanous sequinned panels. Other ideas for evening wear include panne velvet dresses and the wide black self-stripe skirts worn with big, soft, untucked cream satin shirts. Silver mules with interlocking C motifs, tying up the leg, and soft, sequinned evening bags that are adorned with Cs demonstrate a new laid-back glamour.

Cardigans and twinsets are fastened with metal loops instead of with gilt buttons, and the motivation to shop at this end of the market has been changed from 'show' to *luxe*.

The sheepskin bag in the collection is a nod to supermodel hippiedom, while the co-respondent shoe is transmuted into a velvety brown goatskin boot with varnished toecap and small heel. The new Chanel version of the Birkenstock sandal is a reminder that this collection serves a very informed fashion market and style cognoscenti. Chanel always said that 'fashion is what's on the street'.

The collection also features a khaki jersey jacket that is almost a copy of the jersey suits designed by Chanel in 1916. The tweed clothes with the wider shaped skirt are almost verging on the Edwardian but with a touch of the kimono shape to them; they also feature the cardigan 'overhang' that was characteristic of Chanel's first

Chris MOORE

collection. Even the Cruise collection featured lots of denim and even dungarees, bringing up yet again the gender crossover of male/female workclothes mooted during World War I by Gabrielle Chanel herself.

The Haute Couture collection was shown in the famous boutique in the rue Cambon, the well-trodden steps painted with gold stripes for a display of clothes that continue the Eastern theme. The Japanese influence can be seen in the flat sandal with gold-painted feet, in the long tweed suits with wide pleated skirt bordered at the bottom with braid, in the unfastened box jackets with perfectly cut arms and in the loose chain belt worn low around the hip, as it is worn throughout the collection.

The collection's peach woollen suit has an unconventional 'jacket', which is more like a truly luxurious version of a fleece. It has no buttons, just using a satin drawstring at the waist. It is worn with a satin undershirt and has revers and wool patch pockets. The sleeves are slightly shorter than is usual and the skirt is a little swingy. It is worn with open-toe thong sandals in black.

Another outfit that is worn with the same chain belt and black sandals mentioned above consists of a white off-the-shoulder top flaring out over a black full skirt. There are swirls of astrakhan trim round the neck, across the body and around the wrists. Variations on the theme include the black jacket and white satin skirt with black organza bows attached, the long full skirt ending on the ankle bone, and the black asymmetric skirt and sage green satin camisole with gold etruscan disc straps and a belt with matching gold disc.

The cream silk satin dress, which consists of a softly gathered skirt and a camisole of gold bead embroidery by Lesage, and worn with square-cut sandals in gun-metal, and the midnight blue crepe fountain dress, which echoes the fountain necklace from 1997, are unashamedly feminine. The draped form of the midnight blue dress is made in the perfect shape to complement its glittering blue design and the chiffon stole that cascades on either side of it.

The clothes of this collection look perfect and their ultimate effect is provocative – at the same time as the eye finds rest in the beauty of the visual, the intellectual senses are disquieted because they are unfamiliar with the lack of associations. The sum of the parts is the grandeur and simplicity we are now familiar with, in a wholly new incarnation.

NIALL McINERNEY

Since the launch of the new collection, photographed by Sheila Metzner in British *Vogue* under the title 'Shooting Stars' in Autumn 1997, coinciding with the opening of the shop in London and the new boutique in Place Vendôme, Paris, there has been a renewed awareness of the great talent of Chanel and a more informed evaluation of her instinct for the modern. The pieces based on the 1932 exhibition pieces are so astonishingly eternal that, instead of trying to keep her reputation alive by tribute, the job of the house now is to engender ingenuity and creativity in the same spirit.

The star – the eternal symbol of purity and light – is the emblem that Chanel have chosen to represent the way ahead. The new collection includes many variations on the theme of pearls and diamonds. Pearls, of course, have always held a host of meanings associated with Chanel's image. They had a special significance for Mademoiselle Chanel herself; she wore huge ropes of them and they were a predominant feature in her costume jewellery lines. The matelassé idea for bags is translated into diamonds and pearls.

The original diamond star brooches and comet necklaces appear in this collection together with smaller, newer pieces, like the diamond star earrings with detachable comet tails, making them supremely adaptable.

The camellia inspired a watch and necklace, created in 1994 after Mademoiselle's favourite flower – one of her ciphers. The clear pastel stones of the 'Venetians' range, the clover shapes, Celtic symbols and modern rings, show how the hue and shape of these stones resemble the colours of the tweeds – topazes are displayed in the window in autumn and cool sapphires in the summer. This forms a whole new way of buying jewellery, to challenge the traditional ideas.

Creamy pearls with diamonds of pure white nestle against each other in sumptuous matelassé designs. The diamonds emit their splendid rays, while the lustrous pearls seem to capture and hold in the light.

The fringe ring and bracelet and the fountain necklace are incredibly modern pieces of jewellery – they hold both stature and classical gravitas and yet they are witty in their design. The movement of these pieces echoes the grace in the movement of Chanel clothes. Other rings have moving parts bearing either rubies, diamonds or pearls, which also serves to reflect the elegant movement of the clothes. Chanel always maintained that she wished her jewellery to be 'like ribbons

NIALL McINERNEY

on the hands of women, supple and capable of being taken apart'.

The pearl rings with a row of moving diamond stars, the ring with two squares of pavé diamonds that looks like two rings, the chunky modern rings with tiny stone chips, and the bracelet and ring made from zigzags of gold are all truly modern. There are variations on the comet necklace and the magnificent sapphire and diamond Shooting Stars necklaces: the 'Starry Night' collection and Collerette, a new Jazz Age pattern in perfectly matched diamonds and white gold.

The South Sea pearls have a silvery patina of the ocean, the corals an orange-red sheen. The coloured stones are frequently cabochon in a modern cut intended for maximum impact. Mademoiselle Chanel herself, often used stones such as topaz, onyx and rough, nearly uncut, Byzantine shapes.

The Mademoiselle, Première and Matelassé watches all have the characteristic face. The exception is the beautiful Haute Joaillerie – unpriced in the catalogue.

Chanel demonstrated that the way one wore jewellery was just as important, if not more so, than the value it had. She advocated that one must never lose a sense of mischief, a childish attitude, and never give too much emphasis to the status that jewels bring to bear. Chanel felt that jewels should emphasise the wearer's own beauty and not outshine the woman wearing them.

The modernity of the way she used jewellery is perhaps more obvious today than when she designed them, as we can witness that her ideals still hold sway. For Mademoiselle Chanel, jewellery gave a keynote of lightness and lifted the heavy lines of plain, modest clothes. She teamed large pieces with baggy trousers and sweaters at a time when people only wore jewels 'for best', or took them out of the vault for a particular occasion. For her, they were a device, an element in an established style, requiring a fine balance between dark and light. This theme can be found in her decor, cosmetics and perfume packaging, and in her clothes.

'I am led by my taste for what shines to attempt, through jewellery, to reconcile elegance and fashion,' she stated. All elements must work to give a whole impression. Whether a queen or a shopworker, the elements must serve the wearer. How better to accentuate the allure of a woman than with the free spirit of the woman herself?

RIGHT
Nadja Auerman wears classic winter black and white - this striking fur-trimmed cape has all the glamour of the 20s and 30s and is still totally modern.

OPPOSITE
A touch of the bizarre - swirls of astrakhan wrap around the body, over a black full skirt and white off the shoulder top.

NIALL McINERNEY

Haute couture models attired in fantasy confections of flimsy silk and tulle in a tough urban arena.

ENRIQUE BADULESCU

RIGHT *The softly folded Jersey wrap front dress is reminiscent of the original Biarritz collection and the soft domed hat is the perfect foil, historically and aesthetically.*

OPPOSITE *Naomi Campbell holds the new-shape Chanel 2005 bag aloft, to demonstrate its ergonomic body-friendly shape for the new millennium.*

PIERRE VERDY

RIGHT *This low-necked long dress with Etruscan discs at the shoulder strap is exquisitely proportioned, sexy and uncompromising in its overall concept.*

OPPOSITE *Pyjamas with a difference; the tight leg is unexpected, while the jacket is at once utilitarian and decorative in shape, the train from the shoulder demonstrates the point of Haute Couture.*

RIGHT *Sheer black chiffon embroidered with the name Chanel in crazy chaotic fashion alongside immaculate arrangements of draped chiffon and delicate shoestring straps.*

OPPOSITE *Chanel approaches the millennium; contrasting heavy monochrome, sculpted forms and even elongated bell-shapes with ultra-delicate organza flowers with beaded stamens on the finest tulle.*

THIERRY ORBAN

THIERRY ORBAN

François KOLLAR

The sweet smell of success

When Mademoiselle Chanel introduced her most famous and now legendary scent Chanel No5 in 1921, she changed the rules of the game of perfume making for ever. It is impossible to overestimate the impact of No5 either then or over the entire 20th century. The creation of Ernest Beaux, former perfumer to the Court of the Russian Tsars, it was a revolutionary product in every way; not only was it worlds away from the flowery scents of the time, made up by small houses who named them as exotically as they could imagine, but it was a grand and potent concoction, full of aldehydes and a huge amount of Jasmine, one of the most expensive ingredients in perfumery, even today.

Chanel was always different, but 78 years on the status of Chanel No5 is mythical, universal, quite simply it is the biggest selling classic of all time. That she single-handedly shifted the emphasis from the traditional way of selling perfume with the identity given by its creator, to the identity bestowed upon it by the creative spirit of the woman of the century, shows an instinct for communication and marketing which was ahead of her time.

Everyone knows that Marilyn Monroe wore only Chanel No5 to bed, it is well-documented that it was the fifth flacon picked from a selection presented by Beaux, even the bottle has a special place in the history of art, having been exhibited at the Museum of Modern Art in New York. Her impact on fashion and femininity had been so momentous, it was the start of the modern marketing ideal, the eternal hope that some of the allure of the ideal would rub off on the woman who bought it.

Chanel's love affair with high society and a Russian Grand Duke was enough to propel the scent into stratospheric sales alone, but also, the look she advocated, the fresh, wholesome balance of impeccable grooming and uncompromising standards, made for an unbeatable image.

Chanel hardly advertised in the early days, which also compounded the envy of her competitors, its exclusivity emphasised Chanel's guiding principle; less is more. The packaging has hardly changed over time, except to accommodate the manufacturing processes which differ when selling millions, not hundreds. The bottle has changed imperceptibly, but the trademark black and white boxes and label still have the idea of a gentleman's cologne or even a medicinal product, which many contemporary fashion designers have introduced in recent years. But No5 has its place in history, through its importance in Chanel's life, by its cultural importance to the allies, who wanted to buy it during the liberation of Paris and above all, its smell.

The smell of Chanel No5 is so distinctive and unique, despite the fact that it reacts differently on every woman, which makes it a mysterious, Proustian substance, redolent of memory and association, yet never being of any one era. A number whose cabalistic and factual connotations intensifies its cultural symbolism. As Jacques Polge, perfumer for Chanel today says:

'It could have been by Reverdy, when other perfumeurs were preoccupied by names that could have been by Baudelaire'.

Chanel launched other perfume in the 20s and 30s; No22 in 1922, Gardenia, an attempt by Beaux to do the impossible and capture the fragrance of a single flower, Bois des Iles with all the elements of the exotic so hard-sought in the 20s and the infamous Cuir de Russie. These scents are still available from Chanel boutiques, but the scents from 1930, of which there were three, are no longer sold; Une idée, Sycomore and Glamour de Chanel. Later in life, with Henri Robert, she launched No19, for her birthday in 1971.

Henri Robert also created the aftershave lotion, Pour Monsieur, presumably to be sold in the boutiques as an extra, for the man who footed the bill for the couture. The associations of her relationships with important men certainly helped sales. Now Chanel produces several men's fragrances, including Antaeus, Egoiste, Platinum Egoiste and its most recent addition, Allure for men.

Jacques Polge the *nez* at Chanel is responsible for these recent men's aftershaves as well as the perfumes created after her death, notably Coco and Allure. The idea of Coco came about because there was no 'baroque' scent at Chanel. It was inspired by Mademoiselle's affection for Venice and the East and it complements the collection, standing as it does in direct opposition to the floral range of the others. Its inspiration was the photograph of Mademoiselle in a gondola in masculine clothing and full make-up. Its famous advertising campaign with Vanessa Paradis in feathers swinging inside a gilded cage originated from a tiny bird in a gold cage at the rue Cambon apartment.

Allure, by contrast, relates to that intangible contrast so inextricably linked with Gabrielle Chanel, that essence whatever it is that makes a woman attractive and draws us near that seductive element. Allure was the adjective used so frequently for Mademoiselle's appeal and she used it about others. Her personal philosophy of beauty was so much about making the most of oneself, being equal to one's destiny in love, preparing to seduce and be seduced in a way that did not diminish individuality or go so far as to become vulgar.

Today, at the House of Chanel, the quest is still to promote beauty in this way; Jacques Polge says 'it's not a woman, it's a spirit... It is linked with fashion, but it doesn't come out of fashion, more from lasting trends. Because Chanel was famous for total image, total awareness of modernity, we keep away from short-lived trends. You can't create a classic, you just create something that has been in the air for a while and it earns its status.'

Chanel herself understood this perfectly. During the 20s, women were playing with men's clothing, none more so than Gabrielle, of course, but with this role play went a serious usage of cosmetics. Women would delight in the scandalous activity of applying deep red lipstick in public and imitating the silent cinema actresses in their liberal use of khol for the eyes. At first, this was an upper class or *beau monde* habit, but it soon filtered down to ordinary working girls with the *garçonne* haircut, shorter skirts and the Charleston. From her early days in the Music Hall and her experiences at Royallieu, Chanel knew a thing or two about maquillage, although her preference

in her youth was for a bandbox, fresh-scrubbed look, particularly on the beach or out of doors. But in time, she was to favour a balanced make-up which accentuated the dark and light of her face and her special red lipstick, which she would wear for the rest of her life. This Chanel red lipstick was made again by the cosmetics division of the company in the 1970s and is re-released periodically. Its name is Rouge Chanel.

In 1924, with the help of the Wertheimer family, the present day owners of Chanel, she produced cosmetics. She knew so well how to put a white collar on a suit to uplight the face, how to place camellias in the hair to emphasise its dark shine. Her love of the East taught her by Boy Capel surely influenced her grasp of beauty and her interpretation of make-up for the day and night. Her love of sport and knowledge of social ritual influenced her introduction of tanning oil to her cosmetics range, she was, after all, one of the first to display a deep tan and her other products included guest soaps, numerous sport and body creams and always creams and pastes for the hands. Many of Chanel's earliest products from her early catalogues include creams scented with No5, stress lotion, glacial rub for the body and bullets of lipstick, before twist up cases were invented.

Mademoiselle's insistence on the best pigments and ingredients are echoed today, particularly in the development of new products. The new skincare range, Precision, shows the gravitas with which Chanel is investing in the future. It took 10 years to perfect and will radically change the analysis of conditions and well-being. Produced in co-operation with the CEntre de Recherches et Investigations Epidermiques et Sensorielles (CE.R.I.E.S.) it has required a huge investment with a long term view. Such a move would have been praised by Mademoiselle, since she was one of the pioneers of what is today modern skincare. Back in the 20s her ideas were radical, but today, every cosmetics and skincare range reflects the concerns that she had for beauty care then.

Dominique Moncourtois and Heidi Morawetz are the creative duo who bridge the gap between the headline-grabbing circus of the catwalk and the women around the world who buy Chanel make-up. In their studio in the heart of Paris is a table with arrangements of pigments, key colours, packaging and other influences even sequins or fabric. All these things are a springboard for their creativity, in order for them to devise a new colour range, each season.

Like Lagerfeld, they are finding inspiration in technology, particularly new materials, the newest of which change colour when temperature changes occur, but next season, who knows, it could be anything. Their track record together is testament to their success. Together they create winning colours, which appeal to different generations alike, from rouge Coromandel to Rouge Noir and they have the influence to bring back eye liner one season and thick fake tan the next. The women who represent the looks of the season on the catwalk and in magazines are the most powerful symbols of beauty of our times and make ordinary women want to emulate those looks.

The women who have personified the Chanel image through perfume advertising have been some of the most beautiful women ever; Catherine Deneuve, Ali McGraw, Carole Bouquet and now, for Chanel No5, Estella Warren. The man who oversees the ideal is Jacques Helleu, who maintains that the advertising in part is there to take the place of the impeccably turned out *vendeuse*, and that the ideal is presented in terms of art, not just communication.

Chanel's advertising has all the sophistication one would expect. The tradition of a type of glamour born out of a spirit the like of which will never be seen again. It has borne witness to such talent and evocation of past times which are continuing to influence the future. Jean-Paul Goude, Ridley Scott, Helmut Newton, Daniel Jouanneau as well as Nicole Wisneau of *Egoiste* magazine, have all collaborated on work for Chanel. Chanel was the first marque to integrate an image with an intangible; perfume, a spirit, it is now raising it to levels of collectability, yet at the same time it presents a simple self-belief attainable to all women. It stands alone, as she once did, undiminished by the complexity and plurality of modern imagery.

The extent to which her beliefs are fundamental to modern culture, the simplicity and frankness of presentation, the instinct for the monumental statement in the simplest form, are all self-evident as it was when the convent girl, so affected by the contrast of light and dark launched not only her products, but herself into society on her creative brilliance alone. Now, more than ever, with the resources to employ the best talent money can buy, the medium is so truthfully and singularly the message for Chanel, that Monsieur Helleu, guardian of the *image de marque* says nonchalantly 'For Chanel, *c'est normal*'.

Ed FEINGERSCH

Acknowledgments

Jacket Associated Press/Laurent Rebours
Front and Back Endpaper Niall McInerney

6 Courtesy Vogue Paris/ADAGP, Paris and DACS, London 2000
12–13 Private Collection/All Rights Reserved
15 Private Collection/Femina/All Rights Reserved
17 Special Collections, Courtesy of the Fashion Institute of Technology Library, New York
18 The Condé Nast Publications Ltd
19 The Condé Nast Publications Ltd
20 Top Special Collections, Courtesy of the Fashion Institute of Technology Library, New York
20 Bottom Left Special Collections, Courtesy of the Fashion Institute of Technology Library, New York
20 Bottom Right Special Collection, Courtesy of the Fashion Institute of Technology Library, New York
21 Top Left Special Collections, Courtesy of the Fashion Institute of Technology Library, New York
21 Top Right Special Collection, Courtesy of the Fashion Institute of Technology Library, New York
21 Bottom Special Collection, Courtesy of the Fashion Institute of Technology Library, New York
22–23 Topham Picturepoint
25 Hulton Getty Picture Collection
27 The Condé Nast Publications Ltd
28 The Condé Nast Publications Ltd
29 left The Condé Nast Publications Ltd
29 right The Condé Nast Publications Ltd
30 The Condé Nast Publications Ltd
31 left The Condé Nast Publications Ltd
31 right Courtesy Vogue Paris
32 The Condé Nast Publications Ltd
33 The Condé Nast Publications Ltd
34 The Condé Nast Publications Ltd
35 Courtesy Vogue Paris/Arthur O'Neill
36 The Condé Nast Publications Ltd
37 The Condé Nast Publications, Inc/Steichen
38–39 Corbis UK Ltd/UPI
41 The National Magazine Co/ Harpers Bazaar/de Meyer/All Rights Reserved
42 Roger-Viollet/Harlingue-Viollet
43 Chanel Archives/Robert Bresson 1932/All Rights Reserved
46 Corbis-Bettmann/UPI
47 The National Magazine Co/ Harpers Bazaar/de Meyer/All Rights Reserved
48 The National Magazine Co/ Harpers Bazaar/de Meyer/All Rights Reserved
49 The Condé Nast Publications, Inc/Hoyningen-Huene
50 The National Magazine Co/ Harpers Bazaar
51 The Condé Nast Publications Ltd/Cecil Beaton
52 The National Magazine Co/ Harpers Bazaar/Luza-Moral/All Rights Reserved
53 The National Magazine Co/ Harpers Bazaar/Luza-Moral/All Rights Reserved
54 Courtesy Vogue Paris/ Hoyningen-Huene
55 Courtesy Vogue Paris/ Hoyningen-Huene
56 Courtesy Vogue Paris/Andre Kertesz c. Ministère de la Culture, France
57 Roger-Viollet/Harlingue-Viollet
58 Chanel Archives/Robert Bresson 1932/All Rights Reserved
59 Chanel Archives/Robert Bresson 1932/All Rights Reserved
61 Sotheby's London/Courtesy of the Cecil Beaton Archive
63 The National Magazine Co/Harpers Bazaar/François Kollar c. Ministère de la Culture, France
65 The National Magazine Co/ Harpers Bazaar/Coco Chanel
66 The Condé Nast Publications Ltd/Reproduced with kind permision of Hamiltons Gallery/Horst P. Horst
67 The Condé Nast Publications Ltd/All Rights Reserved
68 The Condé Nast Publications Ltd/Reproduced with kind permission of Hamiltons Gallery/ Horst P. Horst
69 The Condé Nast Publications Ltd/Nelson
70 The Condé Nast Publications Ltd/Reproduced with kind permission of Hamiltons Gallery/ Horst P. Horst
71 The National Magazine Co/ Harpers Bazaar/George Platt-Lynes/All Rights Reserved
72 The National Magazine Co/ Harpers Bazaar/George Platt-Lynes/All Rights Reserved
73 The Condé Nast Publications Ltd/With kind permission of Hamiltons Gallery/Horst P. Horst
74 The National Magazine Co/ Harpers Bazaar/Hoyningen-Huene
75 The National Magazine Co/ Harpers Bazaar/François Kollar c. Ministère de la Culture, France
76 The National Magazine Co/ Harpers Bazaar/Man Ray/ c. ADAGP, Paris and DACS, London 2000
77 The Condé Nast Publications Ltd/With kind permission of Hamiltons Gallery/Horst P. Horst
79 NETWORK/Rapho/E Kammerman
81 Advertising Archives/Courtesy of Paul Himmel
82 Advertising Archives/Courtesy of Paul Himmel
83 Courtesy Vogue Paris/Henry Clarke/c. ADAGP, Paris and DACS, London 2000
84 Advertising Archives/Courtesy of Paul Himmel
85 The Condé Nast Publications, Inc/Henry Clarke/c. ADAGP, Paris and DACS, London 2000
86 The Condé Nast Publications, Inc/Henry Clarke/c. ADAGP, Paris and DACS, London 2000
87 Advertising Archives/Courtesy of Paul Himmel
88 The Condé Nast Publications Ltd/Henry Clarke/c. ADAGP, Paris and DACS, London 2000
89 Courtesy Vogue Paris/Henry Clarke/c. ADAGP, Paris and DACS, London 2000
90 The Condé Nast Publications, Inc/Henry Clarke/c. ADAGP, Paris and DACS, London 2000
91 The Condé Nast Publications, Inc/Henry Clarke/c. ADAGP, Paris and DACS, London 2000
93 Magnum Photos/Henri Cartier-Bresson
95 Popperfoto
96 Rex Features/Hatami
97 Popperfoto
98 The Condé Nast Publications, Inc/Henry Clarke/c. ADAGP, Paris and DACS, London 2000
99 Rex Features/Hatami
100 Rex Features/Hatami
101 The Condé Nast Publications, Inc/Henry Clarke/c. ADAGP, Paris and DACS, London 2000
102 Popperfoto
103 Rex Features/Hatami
104 The Condé Nast Publications, Inc/Henry Clarke/c. ADAGP, Paris and DACS, London 2000
105 The National Magazine Co/ Harpers Bazaar/with kind permission from Richard Dormer
106 Rex Features/Hatami
107 Rex Features/Hatami
108–109 Courtesy Vogue Paris/ Tony Kent
111 Hulton Getty Picture Collection
112 Hulton Getty Picture Collection
113 Hulton Getty Picture Collection
114 Courtesy Vogue Paris/Henry Clarke/c. ADAGP, Paris and DACS, London 2000
115 Courtesy Vogue Paris/Mike Reinhardt/JGK, Inc
116 Chanel Archive/Jean-Pierre Ledos/All Rights Reserved
117 Hulton Getty Picture Collection
118 Courtesy Vogue Paris/Mike Reinhardt/JGK, Inc
119 Courtesy Vogue Paris/Mike Reinhardt/JGK, Inc
120–121 Christopher Moore Ltd
123 Christopher Moore Ltd
124 Courtesy Vogue Paris/ Courtesy of Hamiltons Gallery/ Horst P. Horst
126 The Condé Nast Publications Ltd/Bruce Weber
127 The Condé Nast Publications Ltd/Bruce Weber
128 The Condé Nast Publications Ltd/Bruce Weber
129 Courtesy Vogue Paris/ Courtesy of Hamiltons Gallery/ Horst P. Horst
130 Courtesy Vogue Paris/ Courtesy of Hamiltons Gallery/ Horst P. Horst
131 Courtesy Vogue Paris/ Courtesy of Hamiltons Gallery/ Horst P. Horst
132–133 Courtesy Vogue Paris/ Courtesy of Hamiltons Gallery/ Horst P. Horst
134–135 Corbis UK Ltd/BDV
137 Christopher Moore Ltd
139 Christopher Moore Ltd
140 Christopher Moore Ltd
141 Christopher Moore Ltd
142 Christopher Moore Ltd
143 Top Christopher Moore Ltd
143 Bottom Christopher Moore Ltd
144 Rex Features
145 Rex Features
146 Christopher Moore Ltd
147 Christopher Moore Ltd
148 Christopher Moore Ltd
149 Christopher Moore Ltd
150 Christopher Moore Ltd
151 Rex Features
152–153 Associated Press/Michel Euler
155 Christopher Moore Ltd
156 Christopher Moore Ltd
157 Niall McInerney
158 Niall McInerney
160 Niall McInerney
161 Rex Features/Steve Wood
162–163 Courtesy Vogue Paris/ Enrique Badulescu/Art Partner
164 Rex Features
165 Agence France Presse/Pierre Verdy
166 Rex Features
167 Rex Features
168 Sygma/Thierry Orban
169 Sygma/Thierry Orban
170 Association Française pour la diffusion du Patrimoine Photographique c. François Kollar
172 Advertising Archives
173 Chanel
174 Advertising Archives
175 Michael Ochs Archives/ Venice, CA/Ed Feingersh